For Jack Pole
with best wishes
Hamilton Bryson

# MISCELLANEOUS
# VIRGINIA LAW REPORTS
## 1784-1809

*being the reports of*

# CHARLES LEE, JOHN BROWN, DAVID WATSON, & DAVID YANCEY

*edited by*
## W. Hamilton Bryson

**OCEANA PUBLICATIONS, INC.**
**DOBBS FERRY * LONDON * ROME**

Miscellaneous Virginia Law Reports. Bryson, Hamilton.
142 pages. Includes: Table of Abbreviations, Table of Cases, Table of Statutes, List of
Appellate Judges and Index.

ISBN: 0-379-20887-3

New York University's Ingram Documents in Legal History
ISSN: 0894-3303

Manufactured in the United States of America on acid free paper.

## DEDICATION

The Ingram Documents in American Legal History are in memory of my parents, Peter T. and Sarah E. Ingram, whose perception and pursuit of social justice were ahead of their time.

*GLORIA INGRAM ROTH*

# TABLE OF CONTENTS

# PREFACE

Printed law reports of American cases from the early federal period are sparse. Therefore, these recently discovered manuscripts of Virginia cases dating from 1784 to 1809 are published here in the belief that they may shed more light on the law of Virginia and the United States and on the courts whose practitioners included Edmund Randolph, Charles Lee, John Marshall, Bushrod Washington, and others.

In order to aid the reader as much as possible in following the points being made in these terse case reports, modern spelling has been used and modern punctuation has been added. This is also reasonable and appropriate according the rule of *idem sonans*, which is that a word is the oral word not the written word. The words enclosed within square brackets were added by the editor to aid the flow of the reports.

I would like to express my appreciation to E. Lee Shepard, who brought to my attention the existence of the manuscripts of the reports of David Watson and David Yancey, and who gave me other invaluable information and editorial assistance. I would also like to acknowledge the kind assistance of Margaret Cook, Charles T. Cullen, John W. Dudley, Charles Kelly, William Ray, and Emily Jones Salmon. Thanks are also due to Robert P. Kline and Russell W. Updike, who helped with the proofreading, and to Carolyn Riley, who typed the manuscript.

The reports of John Brown are published with the permission of the Virginia State Librarian, and those of Charles Lee with the permission of The Colonial Williamsburg Foundation and the Manuscript Department of the University of Virginia Library; an earlier version of them was printed in the *University of Richmond Law Review*, volume 11, pages 695-741 (1977), which is reprinted here with permission. An earlier version of the introduction was published as "Virginia Manuscript Law Reports" in *Law Library Journal*, volume 82, pages 305-311 (1990), and is reprinted with permission.

Finally I would like to thank the University of Richmond for subsidizing the financial cost of this book.

*W. H. Bryson*
**Richmond, Virginia**
**May 15, 1990**

# TABLE OF ABBREVIATIONS

**Atk**. - John Tracy Atkyns, *Reports* (1765-1768), 3 vols.

**Barnes** - Henry Barnes, *Notes of Cases* (1741).

**Call** - Daniel Call, *Reports of Cases . . . in the Court of Appeals of Virginia* (1801, 1802, 1805, 1833), 6 vols.

**Chan. Rep.** - *Reports . . . in . . . Chancery* (1693-1716), 3 vols.

**Co. Rep.** - Edward Coke, *Reports* (1600-1659), 13 vols.

**Cranch** - William Cranch, *Reports of Cases . . . in the Supreme Court of the United States* (1804-1817), 9 vols.

**Cro. Car.** - George Croke, *Reports* (1657), vol. 3.

**Davis** - John Davies (or Davis), *Reports* (1615).

**Dougl.** - Sylvester Douglas, *Reports* (1782), 4 vols.

**Eng. Rep.** - *The English Reports* (1900-1930), 178 vols.

**Gratt.** - Peachy Ridgway Grattan, *Reports of Cases* (1845-1881), 33 vols.

**Hen. & M.** - William Waller Hening and William Munford, *Reports of Cases . . . in the Supreme Court of Appeals of Virginia* (1808, 1809, 1810, 1811), 4 vols.

**Hening's Statutes** - William Waller Hening, *Statutes at Large . . . of Virginia* (1809-1823), 13 vols.

**Jeff.** - Thomas Jefferson, *Reports of Cases Determined in the General Court of Virginia* (1829).

**Jenk.** - David Jenkins, *Eight Centuries of Reports* (1661).

**Keble** - Joseph Keble, *Reports* (1685).

**Ld. Raym.** - Robert, Lord Raymond, *Reports* (1743), 2 vols.

**Leigh** - Benjamin Watkins Leigh, *Reports of Cases* (1830-1844), 12 vols.

**Lev.** - Cresswell Levinz, *Reports* (1702).

**Munf.** - William Munford, *Reports* (1812-1821), 6 vols.

**P. Wms.** - William Peere Williams, *Reports* (1740-1749), 3 vols.

**Rand.** - Peyton Randolph, *Reports of Cases . . . in the Court of Appeals of Virginia* (1823-1829), 6 vols.

**Shepherd's Statutes** - Samuel Shepherd, *Statutes at Large of Virginia* (1835-1836), 3 vols.

**Sid.** - Thomas Siderfin, *Reports* (1783-1784).

**Strange** - John Strange, *Reports* (1755), 2 vols.

**T. Raym.** - Thomas Raymond, *Reports* (1696).

**Term Rep.** - Charles Durnford and Edward Hyde East, *Term Reports* (1787-1800), 8 vols.

**U.S.** - United States Supreme Court Reports.

**Va.** - Virginia Reports. [The early privately published reports of Virginia appellate court cases were renumbered and added to the beginning of this series of official reports.]

**1 Va. Cas.** - William Brockenbrough and Hugh Holmes, *A Collection of Cases Decided by the General Court of Virginia* (1815).

**2 Va. Cas.** - William Brockenbrough, *Virginia Cases or Decisions of the General Court of Virginia* (1826).

**Va. Mag. Hist. Biog.** - *Virginia Magazine of History and Biography.*

# TABLE OF ABBREVIATIONS

**VCD** - Robert Thomas Barton, ed., *Virginia Colonial Decisions: The Reports by Sir John Randolph and by Edward Barradall* (1909), 2 vols.

**Vent.** - Peyton Ventris, *Reports* (1696).

**Wash.** - Bushrod Washington, *Reports of Cases . . . in the Court of Appeals of Virginia* (1798, 1799), 2 vols.

**Wilson K.B.** - George Wilson, *Reports* (1770-1775), 2 vols.

**Wm. & Mary Q.** - *William and Mary Quarterly.*

**Wms. Saund.** - Edmund Saunders, *Reports* (ed. by J. Williams, 1799), 2 vols.

**Wythe** - George Wythe, *Decisions of Cases in Virginia by the High Court of Chancery* (2d ed. 1852).

# Table of Cases Cited in Opinions

# Table of Statutes Cited in Opinions

# Table of Cases Reported

# APPELLATE JUDGES DURING THE TIME
## OF THESE REPORTS

John Blair
Francis Taliaferro Brooke
Cuthbert Bullitt
Paul Carrington
Richard Cary
William Roscow Wilson Curl
Bartholomew Dandridge
William Fleming
James Henry
Hugh Holmes
Joseph Jones
Peter Lyons
James Mercer
William Nelson
Robert Carter Nicholas
Richard Parker
Edmund Pendleton
Joseph Prentis
Spencer Roane
Archibald Stuart
Creed Taylor
Henry Tazewell
St. George Tucker
John Tyler
Benjamin Waller
Edmund Winston
George Wythe

# INTRODUCTION

The common law is in its essence case law. And this is so fundamentally believed by the practitioners of the common law that, whatever their heads may tell them about the constitutional place of a statute to alter the common law, they cannot in their hearts accept the obvious meaning of a statute unless it is corroborated and expounded by a judge by means of a formal judicial opinion in a lawsuit. Reports of cases are and shall always be the foundation of the law. Moreover, the written reports of cases are the life blood of the common law because over time the memory fades and because different people have different memories of the same events and lawsuits and judicial opinions.

In colonial Virginia, only five sets of law reports are known to have been made, although almost all of the printed English law reports are known to have been present and available.[1] These Virginia reports were compiled by Sir John Randolph, Edward Barradall, William Hopkins, Thomas Jefferson, and John Randolph, son of Sir John.

Sir John Randolph's manuscript reports,[2] which cover the period October 1729 to April 1732, were used by Thomas Jefferson, and their existence was generally known in Virginia legal circles around 1800.[3] They were published by Robert T. Barton in 1909.[4]

The manuscript reports of Edward Barradall[5] covering the period 1733 to 1741 were also known to Jefferson. J. W. Ran-

---

1  W. H. Bryson, *Census of Law Books in Colonial Virginia* (1978), pp. xii, 1-17.

2  R. E. Nance, "Sir John Randolph" in W. H. Bryson, *Virginia Law Reporters Before 1880* (1977), pp. 69-70

3  Letter of Merit Moore Robinson to John Robinson, May 9, 1811, Swem Library at the College of William and Mary (the writer of the letter believed that Edmund Randolph had the book, and he was trying to borrow or copy it).

4  R. T. Barton, Virginia Colonial Decisions: The Reports by Sir John Randolph and by Edward Barradall (1909). [hereinafter cited as VCD].

5  R.E. Nance, "Edward Barradall" in W.H. Bryson, Virginia Law Reporters

dolph proposed in 1852 to publish Barradall's reports, [6] but this was not accomplished until 1909.

William Hopkins compiled a series of cases dating from at least October 1731 to April 1733. There were at least two manuscript volumes, but they are now lost. Jefferson used them shortly before Independence when they were in the possession of the last colonial attorney general, John Randolph (d. 1784), the son of Sir John Randolph. There are several extracts or fragments of cases abridged from Hopkins's reports in the Library of Congress in a manuscript book entitled "Virginia Reports" which also contains Sir John Randolph's reports. [7]

The fourth set of colonial Virginia reports was made by Thomas Jefferson when he was a young man engaged in the practice of law in Williamsburg on the eve of Independence. Jefferson extracted four cases from the manuscript of Sir John Randolph, twenty-six from Barradall, and one very short case from Hopkins. Jefferson followed these in his own manuscript book with eleven cases dating from October 1768 to October 1772. Jefferson's *Reports* were published in 1829, after his death, by his grandson, Thomas Jefferson Randolph. [8]

From later citations, we know that John Randolph, the son of Sir John Randolph, also made manuscript reports of cases. (He was the last colonial attorney general; he died in England in 1784, but his body was returned to Virginia for burial in Williamsburg.) Unfortunately his manuscript books have been lost, but several of the cases reported by him were cited

---

Before 1880 (1977), pp. 71-74.

6  See the publisher's notice in G. Wythe, Decisions of Cases (2d ed. by B. B. Minor, 1852), pp. [v], [xliv]. *See note 4.*

7  R. T. Barton, *Virginia Colonial Decisions: The Reports by Sir John Randolph and by Edward Barradall*, vol.1 pp. 1, 12, 184 (1909); T. Jefferson, *Reports of Cases*, preface (1829); C. Robinson, "Of Lawyers in Virginia between 1704 and 1737", *Va. Law Jour.*, vol. 1, pp. 191, 193 (1877).

8  G. M. Curtis, III, "Thomas Jefferson," in W. H. Bryson, *Virginia Law Reporters Before 1880* (1977), pp. 75-84.

in later cases. *Steger v. Moseley* (1773), "October, 1773, M.S. Rep. by J. Randolph, 2 vol. page 232," was cited in argument by his son, Edmund Randolph[9], and by Judges Roane and Pendleton in *Wallace v. Taliaferro*, 6 Va. (2 Call) 450, 470, 487 (1800). *Wallace v. Taliaferro* at pages 450, 470, and 488 also cites *Bronaugh v. Cocke* and at page 470 *Smyth v. Lucas*, these last two cases also being found in the younger John Randolph's reports. The case of *Dobson v. Taylor* (1755), which was found at page 77 of John Randolph's reports, was brought to the attention of the Supreme Court of Appeals by Edmund Randolph in the case of *Claiborne v. Henderson* (1809), and it was discussed by the court and printed in a footnote by the reporters.[10]

The bar was particularly in need of reports of Virginia case decisions after Independence when appeals to the Privy Council in England were no longer allowed and English judges were no longer the ultimate authority on Virginia law. It is also to be noted that after 1776, the judges of the higher courts were all former members of the bar, and thus the level of the opinions of the court improved considerably. However, it was not until 1795 that the first reports of any Virginia cases were printed and published; these were the cases of George Wythe from the High Court of Chancery, an intermediate appellate court that also had original jurisdiction.[11]

Charles Lee, who later became the United States Attorney General from 1795 to 1801, compiled a small collection of Virginia cases while he was in practice in Alexandria. He reported cases from many different courts though not many from any single one. There are cases from the Virginia Court of Appeals, the General Court, the High Court of Chancery, the District Court of Fredericksburg, and the Federal Court.

---

9   See generally J. J. Reardon, *Edmund Randolph* (1974).

10   13 Va. (3 Hen. & M.) 322 at 335-337, 362, 374-375, 384 (1809).

11   E. L. Shepard, "George Wythe" in W. H. Bryson, *Virginia Law Reports Before 1880* (1977), pp. 90-95.

During the period covered by Charles Lee's reports, April 1784 to January 1794, there were no reports of Virginia cases in print. Whether he was aware of the existence of the manuscript collections of colonial Virginia cases is unknown, nor is it known whether he knew that Bushrod Washington, John Marshall, and St. George Tucker were making notes of cases at the same time that he was. Lee thus had no printed Virginia reports to use, but he cited numerous English reports and several English treatises: reports of cases by Lord Raymond, Saunders, Keble, Siderfin, Levinz, Ventris, Croke, T. Raymond, Jenkins, Wilson, Strange, Peere Williams, *Chancery Reports*, Atkyns, *Term Reports*, Coke, Davis, Barnes, and Burrow; Matthew Bacon's *New Abridgment of the Law*; *Coke Upon Littleton*; Sir William Blackstone, *Commentaries on the Laws of England*; and John Joseph Powell, *Essay on the Law of Contracts and Agreements* (1790).

John Brown was the clerk of the Court of Appeals of Virginia from 1785 to 1810. There were no printed reports of Virginia cases when John Brown began making his notes of cases in the Court of Appeals, but by October 1799, when his last surviving note was made, George Wythe's reports and both volumes of Bushrod Washington's reports had been published. We have no way of knowing the dates of the cases in Brown's lost second volume, but they may well have continued until his death in 1810. Conway Robinson cited six cases from a third but now lost volume of cases from the General Court, cases dating from 1788 to 1794.[12] Brown made notes of legal points decided in the Court of Appeals of Virginia concentrating on appellate procedure and court costs. They were no doubt for his own personal future use as clerk of that court. He was not acting as either an advocate or as a judge, and thus his reports contain no references to printed materials other than Virginia statutes. Occasionally, he notes oral references to other cases that had been recently decided by the Court of Appeals. All of them are earlier than Bushrod

---

12 See below.

Washington's first volume which was printed in 1798, so that could not have been the source of the information.

David Watson, a prominent lawyer and politician in Louisa County, Virginia, compiled a series of case reports from the county courts of Louisa, Goochland, and Fluvanna and the District Court of Charlottesville. They were begun in November 1799, after the publication of George Wythe's reports and both volumes of Washington's *Reports*. While Watson was making his compilation, the last case in which is dated August 1809, the first three volumes of reports by Daniel Call and the first two by William Waller Hening and William Munford were issued to the public. Watson, who practiced only in the county courts and in the district court in his neighborhood, cited cases in the first volume of Washington and the first volume of Call. A reference to volume one of Hening and Munford was added later to the end of his report of *Ford v. Gardner* (1799). Watson also referred to St. George Tucker's 1803 edition of Blackstone's *Commentaries*; Isaac Espinasse, *Nisi Prius*; and John Fon blanque, *Treatise of Equity*.

David Yancey, a close friend and neighbor of Watson, also kept notes of cases. Yancey's brief collection of cases in the District Court of Charlottesville dating from April 1804 to April 1806 was begun after the appearance of the works by Wythe and Washington and the first two volumes of Call's *Reports*. Yancey's cases cite authority from the first volumes of Washington and of Call and from the English reports by Wilson, Lord Raymond, and Douglas. Yancey also refers to Tucker's edition of Blackstone's *Commentaries*.

St. George Tucker compiled a series of reports of cases dating from 1786 to 1811; from 1788 until 1811, Tucker was a judge and thus was reporting cases argued before him.[13] In 1825, Daniel Call wrote to Tucker for permission to print a selection of opinions from his manuscript reports. The felicitous

---

13  Tucker's reports are now in the Swem Library of the College of William and Mary and are being prepared for publication. See C. T. Cullen, "St. George Tucker" in W. H. Bryson, *Virginia Law Reports Before 1880* (1977) pp. 96-105.

result was the publication in 1833 of volumes four, five, and six of Call's *Reports*; most, if not all, of the cases were from Tucker's books.[14]

John Marshall also reported cases when he was in practice in Virginia. It is truly unfortunate that Marshall's manuscript reports have been lost. However, fifteen of these cases dating from 1790 were printed in Call's *Reports*, volume 3, pages 506-599, and Marshall's report of *Turberville v. Self*, 8 Va. (4 Call) 580, 590 (1795), was also used by Call.[15]

Even after the printing of the Virginia reports was begun, there was a need to resort to the manuscript cases. In 1811, after ten volumes of Virginia cases had appeared, Merit Moore Robinson, a Norfolk attorney, was trying to get access to Sir John Randolph's reports and St. George Tucker's notes of cases.[16] In the case of *White v. Jones*[17] in 1792, John Marshall arguing for the appellee and Edmund Pendleton, president of the Court of Appeals, discuss the case of *Chew v. Stevens* (1736) which was reported by Barradall and Jefferson.[18] Pendleton noted that since it had not been published, it was "known only to very few of the profession; and perhaps, hardly to any practicing in the country only." (Marshall and Pendleton also mentioned the case of *Hambleton v. Wells*,[19] which had been decided by Pendleton only sixteen months before, but it was no doubt cited from memory rather than in reference to a manuscript.)

---

14  Letter of Daniel Call to St. George Tucker, April 27, 1825, Swem Library, College of William and Mary; D. Call, *Reports*, vol. 4, pp. [v], xxviii (1833).

15  C. F. Hobson, ed., *The Papers of John Marshall*, vol. 5, pp. 473-474 (1987); J. W. Wallace, *The Reporters* (4th ed. 1882), p. 590, note 3.

16  Letters of May 9, 1811, and September 3, 1811, from Merit Moore Robinson to John Robinson, Swem Library, College of William and Mary. I would like to thank E. Lee Shepard for these references and for the next.

17  8 Va. (4 Call) 253, 257 (1792).

18  Legan, lessee of Chew v. Stevens, 2 VCD B166, Jeff. 30 (1736).

19  8 Va. (4 Call) 213 (1791); this case is also reported in Brown's reports, *infra*. Note that the fourth volume of Call's *Reports* was not published until 1833.

# INTRODUCTION

A manuscript report of *Hambleton v. Wells* (1791) was cited in St. George Tucker's 1803 edition of Blackstone's *Commentaries*.[20] The case was also remembered by counsel for the appellant in *Witherington v. M'Donald*[21] in 1807:

> Judge Roane inquired whether the case of *Hambleton v. Wells* had ever been reported. On being answered in the negative, he observed that he had a manuscript note of it copied from one in the handwriting of Judge Pendleton, and, if no better report could be had, he would submit that to the inspection of the court; of its accuracy, he had no doubt, though it was but a brief note.

It was published in a footnote by the reporters. Judge Spencer Roane, in his opinion in the controversial case of *Hunter v. Fairfax's Devisee*, 15 Va. (1 Munf.) 218 at 225-227 (1810), cited three earlier Virginia cases[22] which had not yet been printed.

*Berryman v. Booth* (1734)[23] in Edward Barradall's reports was cited by Judge Dabney Carr in 1835 in his opinion in *Worsham v. Worsham*, 32 Va. (5 Leigh) 589 at 592 (1835). William Green mentioned that he had consulted *Taylor v. Graves* (1736)[24] as found in Barradall's reports in his celebrated argument in *Moon v. Stone*, 60 Va. (19 Gratt.) 130 at 320, 321 (1869). Conway Robinson cited seven cases from the manuscript reports of Barradall. They are *Rose v. Cooke*, 2 VCD B192, B229 (1736); *Brooking v. Dudley*, 2 VCD B256 (1737); *Edwards v. Bridger*, 2 VCD B117 (1740); *Micou v. Corbin*, 2 VCD

---

20  Vol. 3, p. 261, note 10 (1803).

21  Witherington v. M'Donald, 11 Va. (1 Hen. & M.) 306, 307 (1807).

22  Reed v. Reed, 15 Va. (1 Munf.) 611 (1805); Marshall v. Conrad, 9 Va. (5 Call) 364 (1805); Commonwealth v. Bristow, 10 Va. (6 Call) 60 (1806). I would like to thank Professor John Paul Jones for these references.

23  2 VCD B42.

24  2 VCD B56.

B37 (1733); *Murdock v. Thornton*, 2 VCD B33 (1733); *Spicer v. Pope*, 2 VCD B232 (1736); and *Winston v. Henry*, 2 VCD B213 (1736).[25]

Robinson also cited from John Brown's lost volume of reports of cases in the General Court *Graham, adm'x v. Graham, adm'r* (1788), *Jones v. Goode* (1789), *Brownlow v. Custis* (1789), *Bird v. Scott* (1791), *Johnson v. Braxton* (1792), and *Bradley v. Barnett* (1794).[26]

St. George Tucker's manuscript reports were relied upon in the following cases. *Blount v. Gee* (1805)[27] was cited in *Dilliard v. Tomlinson*, 15 Va. (1 Munf.) 183 at 197 (1810). *Triplett v. Dunlop* (1806)[28] was cited in his argument by Call in *Templeman v. Steptoe*, 15 Va. (1 Munf.) 339 at 349 (1810). *Sorrell's Case* (1786)[29] and *Bailey's Case* (1798)[30] were cited in *Commonwealth v. Myers*, 3 Va. (1 Va. Cas.) 188 (1811). *Dudley v. Crump* (1786) was cited in his argument by William Green in *Moon v. Stone*, 60 Va. (19 Gratt.) 130 at 321 (1869). *Clayton v. Latham*, "1 Tuck. MSS. 388," was cited by Green in "Stare Decisis," 14 *Am. L. Rev.* 609 at 645, note 8 (1880). *Dunlop v. Harris* (1804)[31] was cited by Tucker's son, Henry St. G. Tucker in his *Notes on Blackstone's Commentaries* (1826), book 2, page 442, and in his *Commentaries on the Laws of Virginia* (1831), volume 1, book 2, page 336.

In 1824, a judge of the Court of Appeals cited[32] a manuscript opinion in the possession of Daniel Call in the case of

---

25   C. Robinson, *Practice in the Courts of Law and Equity in Virginia*, vol. 1, pp. 161, 288, 123, 404, 76, 137, 527 (1832); vol. 2, pp. 98, 121 (1835).

26   C. Robinson, *Practice in the Courts of Law and Equity in Virginia*, vol. 1, pp. 390, 592, 535-536, 657, 551, 616 (1832).

27   Later reported in 9 Va. (5 Call) 481 (1805).

28   Later reported *sub nom.* Triplett v. Wilson et al., 10 Va. (6 Call) 47 (1806).

29   Later reported in 3 Va. (1 Va. Cas.) 253 (1786).

30   Later reported in 3 Va. (1 Va. Cas.) 258 (1798).

31   Later reported in 9 Va. (5 Call) 16 (1804).

32   Munford v. Overseers of the Poor, 23 Va. (2 Rand.) 313 at 316 (1824). Note this reporter was Peyton Randolph, son of Edmund Randolph; see R. G. Tavenner,

*Braxton v. Winslow* (1791). Although Call's manuscript version of this case was later published in 1833,[33] it does not seem to have come from St. George Tucker because Call's letter requesting permission to see Tucker's manuscripts was dated 1825.[34] In his argument in *Martin v. Stover*, 6 Va. (2 Call) 514 at 518 (1801), Call cites the case of *Calvert v. Bowdoin* (1791) from a "M.S. Rep. in this Court."[35] Call goes on to copy it as a footnote to the principal case. Call and Wickham in their arguments in *Ross v. Overton*, 7 Va. (3 Call) 309 at 312, 313, 316 (1802), cited manuscript reports of *Deane v. Cunliffe* (1797) and *Brown v. Ross*.

This book presents to the general public the reports of Charles Lee, John Brown, David Watson, and David Yancey. The search continues for the lost reports.

The two lost volumes of William Hopkins from the 1730s were last used by Thomas Jefferson around 1775. These two books were probably acquired by Sir John Randolph and passed to his son John, who owned them when Jefferson consulted them. The younger John died in 1784, and they probably then passed to his son Edmund Randolph.

The younger John Randolph compiled two volumes of reports in the 1760s and 1770s. They were last used when his son Edmund cited from them in 1809.

John Brown made a second volume of notes of cases in the Court of Appeals that was a continuation of the volume that is printed here. This second volume may well have covered cases from 1799 until his death in 1810; he was clerk of the Court of Appeals from 1785 to 1810. It was probably a small book, as volume one was. There is no known reference to it, but one may guess that Conway Robinson and William Green

"Peyton Randolph" in W. H. Bryson, *Virginia Law Reporters Before 1880* (1977), pp. 47-48.

33 Braxton v. Winslow, 8 Va. (4 Call) 308 (1791).

34 See above.

35 *I.e.* Court of Appeals.

saw it. Brown also compiled notes of cases in the General Court from 1788 to 1794; he was clerk of this court from 1781 to 1794. Considering the nature of his surviving reports, it is likely that he ceased to report cases from the General Court when he ceased to be its clerk. This lost volume was used by Conway Robinson in preparing a book which was published in 1832.

John Marshall reported cases from the time that he was in practice in Virginia, 1781 to 1800. This lost manuscript was last seen by Daniel Call, his brother-in-law, who copied a case into volume four of his own *Reports*, which was published in 1833.

## The Courts

The court structure of Virginia immediately following Independence in 1776 was a slight modification of the former colonial system. The first level of courts included the county courts and the borough (or corporation or hustings) courts staffed respectively by the justices of the peace and the mayor, recorder, and aldermen. Above these courts were the General Court, the High Court of Chancery, and the Court of Admiralty; these courts had both appellate and original jurisdiction. The highest court in Virginia was the Court of Appeals, which was created to take the place of the Privy Council in London. The judges of the General Court, the High Court of Chancery, and the Court of Admiralty also sat together as the Court of Appeals.[36]

In 1788, the appellate courts were reorganized. The Court of Admiralty was abolished when its jurisdiction was transferred to the new federal courts upon the ratification of the Constitution of the United States. The Court of Appeals was reorganized so that its judges did not sit in any other court, and its jurisdiction over criminal appeals was taken away. The General Court thus became the court of last resort in

[36]  Hening's Statutes, vol. 9, pp. 202-206, 389-399, 401-419, 522-525.

criminal matters. A new level of courts was erected between the county and borough courts and the General Court; these were called district courts, and they were staffed by two judges of the General Court, who went out from Richmond on circuit. Appeals lay from the county and borough courts to the district courts and from them to the General Court in Richmond.[37]

---

37 Hening's Statutes, vol. 12, pp. 467-474, 730-770, 775-776; see generally M. V. Nelson, *A Study of Judicial Review in Virginia 1789-1928* (1947), pp. 13-53.

# CHARLES LEE

Charles Lee, the son of Henry Lee and Lucy Grymes Lee, brother of "Light-Horse Harry" Lee, was born in 1758 at Lee-sylvania, Prince William County, Virginia. He entered Princeton in 1770 and received his B.A. in 1775 and an M.A. in 1778. In the next year he was reading law in Philadelphia, and in 1781 he was licensed to practice in Virginia.[1] From 1781 to 1795 Charles Lee practiced law in Alexandria. He was quite successful, having cases in all the courts of northern Virginia. It was during this period that he compiled these reports of Virginia cases. He was also politically active, holding the Virginia appointment of Naval Officer of the South Potomac from 1784 until 1789, when the position was suppressed upon the adoption of the Federal Constitution. He was the customs collector for the port of Alexandria from August 1789 to 1793, and from then until 1795, he represented Fairfax County in the Virginia House of Delegates.[2]

Charles Lee was an old personal friend of George Washington and shared his ardent Federalist views. Lee was appointed United States Attorney General in November, 1795, and was continued in office by John Adams. He remained the Attorney General until the Federalists lost political power in 1801. He was a close friend of John Marshall, who had the same political and judicial outlook. Lee retired from the active political scene and devoted the rest of his life to his private law practice. He was counsel in *Marbury v. Madison* and aided in the defenses of Aaron Burr and Samuel Chase.[3] He

1  *Dictionary of American Biography* (1933), vol. 11, pp. 101-102; Virginia Historical Society Mss. 1, L 5113, a6, Mss. 2, M 3817, al.

2  E. G. Swem and J. W. Williams, *Register of the General Assembly of Virginia* (1918), pp. 39, 41, 44; *The South in the Building of the Nation* (1909), vol. 12, pp. 70-71.

3  R. Sobel, *Biographical Directory of the United States Executive Branch* (1971), p. 209; W. H. Bryson, "Charles Lee" in *Virginia Law Reporters Before 1880* (1977), pp. 85-86.

died at his home in Fauquier County, Virginia, on June 24, 1815.

## LEE'S REPORTS

Charles Lee reported cases from many different courts though not many from any single one. There are cases from the Virginia Court of Appeals, the General Court, the High Court of Chancery, the District Court of Fredericksburg, and the Federal Court. They date from April 1784 to 1794 or 1795.

Lee's reports have been transcribed from two sources. The earlier cases, from the beginning through *Anonymous,* were found in a largely unused notebook which is now in the possession of Colonial Williamsburg, Inc.[4] The later cases, *Alexander v. Murray* to the end, were found at the end of a notebook entitled "Suits pending 1st Jany. 1794."[5] This latter manuscript is not as neat in hand or in grammar as the former; this suggests that we have here only rough notes taken in court. Judging from the presence of a title page in the Williamsburg manuscript, it was apparently intended to be the finished product. However, it is unlikely that Lee ever intended to publish it. Lee's reports were first published in the *University of Richmond Law Review,* volume 11, pages 695-711 (1977).

---

[4]  I would like to thank The Colonial Williamsburg Foundation for giving permission to publish its *Charles Lee Notebook of Virginia Cases.* Another copy is in the Virginia State Library, MS. 21779b; this copy was kindly brought to my attention by Charles T. Cullen and John W. Dudley.

[5]  I would like to thank the Manuscript Department of the University of Virginia Library for giving permission to publish its *Register of Law Cases by Charles Lee (1794)* (Accession No. 850).

# Cases adjudged in the General Court from the year 1783 to the year [    ].[6] Compiled by Charles Lee. L.A.

April 1784

## Desmarais assignee v. Jones

[This was a] motion for trial out of course under [the] Act of Assembly of 1779[7] in favor of foreigners.

Curia. The assignee stands in the shoes of the original obligee, and in this case, he being a citizen, the motion must be dismissed.

## Turner v. Turner[8]

Appeal; Slaves.

[The] question [was] whether the slave law of 1758[9] be confined by the preamble or to have general operation.

[The] Chief Justice and Judge Lyons [were] of [the] opinion that it was not to be confined by the preamble. Judge Mercer [held] contra. [It was] adjourned for further argument.

## Finnie v. Gilbert

Appeal from the Court of Hustings at Williamsburg.

H. Tazewell for [the] appellant.

The exception that I rely on is to the declaration's not averring that the cause of action did arise within the jurisdiction of the court, the Court of Hustings being an inferior court: 2 Raym. 795, Stanian v. Davis. *Id.* 1310, Sir Thomas Cooke, Winford v. Powell. 1 Saund. 73, Peacok v. Bell. As to local actions 3 Keb. 677, Harvey v. Holland.[10]

---

6  Date left blank in the manuscript.

7  Hening's Statutes, vol. 10, p. 203.

8  Further proceedings in this case are reported in 1 Va. (1 Wash.) 139 (1792) and 8 Va. (4 Call) 234 (1792).

9  Hening's Statutes, vol. 7, pp. 237-239.

10  Stanian v. Davis, 2 Ld. Raym. 795, 92 Eng. Rep. 31 (K.B. 1702); Winford v.

Nothing is to be intended within the jurisdiction of an inferior court unless [it be] averred. 1 Sid. 95, 3 Lev. 243, 1 Vent. 28, Cro. Car. 571, Thos. Raym. 63.[11]

Edmund Randolph contra arguendo.

A court which has jurisdiction over transitory actions is not limited and no averment in such case [is] requisite. The Court of Hustings [is] a court of record and [is] not within the description of an inferior court.

Judge Mercer. The Court of Hustings having general jurisdiction, the matter [is] to be intended within it and need not to be averred. Being a court of record, it cannot be deemed an inferior court according to the British ideas as no writ of false judgment lies therefrom.

Judge Lyons. Transitory actions need only to be so laid within the jurisdiction that they may be intended.

[The] Chief Justice [was] of the same opinion.

The appeal [was] dismissed.

October 1784

### Gault et ux. v. Hornsby et al.

Supersedeas; Debt.

A principal obligor and the executor of another obligor cannot be sued in the same writ if [they are] bound jointly and severally.

---

Powell, 2 Ld. Raym. 1310, 92 Eng. Rep. 357 (K.B. 1712); Peacock v. Bell, 1 Wms. Saund. 73, 85 Eng. Rep. 84 (K.B. 1667); Harvey v. Holland, 3 Keble 677, 84 Eng. Rep. 948 (K.B. 1676).

11  Littlebury v. Wright, 1 Sid. 95, 82 Eng. Rep. 992 (K.B. 1662); Adney v. Vernon, 3 Lev. 243, 83 Eng. Rep. 671 (1685); Barkley v. Paine, 1 Vent. 28, 86 Eng. Rep. 20 (K.B. 1669); Bulley v. Hubbins, Cro. Car. 571, 79 Eng. Rep. 1090 (K.B. 1639); Littleboy v. Wright, T. Raym. 63, 83 Eng. Rep. 35 (K.B. 1663).

### Stringer v. Stringer

Supersedeas in ejectment.

The error assigned was that habere facias possessionem was adjudged to issue after the term had expired. Curia. This is fatal and [the] judgment must be reversed. Then another question arose whether court would order restitution and Jenk. 58[12] was cited in favor of it. Mr. Mason opposed the restitution a year having elapsed since execution was made but this objection was considered insufficient and restitution [was] ordered.

### Copland's exrs. v. Dunn

Detinue; Limitation.

Curia. The act of limitations may be given in evidence on the plea of non detinet or non debet.

### Clarke v. LaFarge

Evidence.

A deposition not objected to at the time of taking it by him on whose behalf it was taken shall be evidence at the trial.

### Hedges v. Cogbill

Evidence.

The assignors of a bond [are] not admitted to prove anything relative to the payment of it, being interested as ultimately though not immediately liable.

### Shore & Co. v. Ferguson

Book debts.

The law of 1779[13] concerning book debts for goods etc. began to operate in May 1780 and continued in force till 1st January 1781; [it] was suspended by an act of the June session

12  Case 7, Jenk. 57, 58, 145 Eng. Rep. 41 (C.P.).
13  Hening's Statutes, vol. 10, p. 133.

1781 from the said 1st January 1781 till the end of the session that should open the courts which happened to be till January 1782, since which it continued in force till May 1783, when it was again suspended till October 1783, since which it has been in full force.

### Brown v. Bailey

Ejectment; Evidence.

Some of the jury [were] admitted to prove the malfeasance of the officers, jury, and themselves as part of the jury in making an inquisition for docking the entail of certain lands.

### Southerland v. England

Appeal; Evidence.

Hearsay being admitted as evidence but not appearing to be in support of direct testimony, the judgment for this cause was reversed.

### Burrow v. Burrow

Detinue; Fraud.

The defendant was present at an arbitration between the plaintiff and his father, and having a deed for certain slaves from the father, did not communicate it to the plaintiff or arbitrators, and these very slaves were awarded to the plaintiff, for which slaves the present action was brought. [The] verdict and judgment [were] for the plaintiff.

### Hedges v. Pegram

Motion; Practice.

A distringas appearing to be irregularly returned was quashed. The court have exercised the right of quashing all executions for irregularity. 2 Wilson 394.[14] But notice must be given to the parties interested in the usual form of the motions for such purposes.

---

14  Hole v. Finch, 2 Wilson K.B. 393, 95 Eng. Rep. 880 (C.P. 1769).

### Newsum v. Davis

Debt; Officers.

The defendant was assistant quartermaster-general and took up goods, for which he gave his bond to the plaintiff the goods being for the public service. [He was] held liable to pay out of his private funds; [the] verdict [was] for [the] plaintiff, and the tobacco [was] estimated at the average price through the Commonwealth. A full court [heard the case].

### Tarte v. Shute

Case; Book debts.

[The] question [was] whether on a store account the articles in which are older than six months, an assumpsit after the account became older than six months but within six months before the bringing of the suit might be given in evidence. [The] court was of opinion [that] it might not, being contrary to the act of 1779[15], but Judge Dandridge differed from the court, and the bar was dissatisfied. However, so it was adjudged.

### Downing v. Nutt

Ejectment; Maxim.

"Possession of part is possession of the whole" applies only to such cases where there is a social possession and not an actual occupation of one to the exclusion of another.

### Dade v. Dade

Ejectment; Special Verdict.

The plaintiff's title was derived from a conveyance of lease and release, the lease [was] dated the 30th May and the release [was] dated the 21st May in the same year, and the only objection to the title was the date of the lease being subsequent to the release.

15  Hening's Statutes, vol. 10, p. 133.

It was argued by H. Tazewell for the plaintiff that the lease and release should operate as a covenant to stand seised to uses. [He] cited 1 Ven. 27[16]. Ut res magis valeat quam pereat. 2 Wilson 75,[17] 333. Deeds of lease and release of a remainder [are] to operate as a covenant to stand seised to uses.

It was argued on the other side by T. Mason for the defendant first that, the lease being void, the release could not operate upon it. 1 Mod. 162. Lit. sect. [ ] Secondly, a privity between lessor and lessee at the time of release [is] necessary. Co. Lit. 273b. This being wanting, the conveyance [was] of no effect.

J. Baker in reply for the plaintiff [argued that] if a grant cannot pass literally, it shall pass otherwise if possible. Co. Lit. 103b, 2 Bac. 666. [He] observed that Hobart and Coke had said that the dates are immaterial and deeds [are] to take effect from livery. [He] cited 1 Vent. 35, 107. Also the defects remedied as to the dates by the Act of Assembly 1748[18] and by the acknowledgment in court.

The court were inclined for the plaintiff but [it was] adjourned for another argument. Afterwards the parties came to an agreement [out of court].

### Cocke's Exrs. v. Linton

Appeal; Paper Money; See the various acts touching paper money.

The appellants sued the appellee in the year 1779 in the County Court of Prince William upon a bond conditioned with the payment of a certain sum in sterling money. Pending the suit, on the 2d day of October 1781, the defendants paid into court the amount of the debt in the condition computed

---

16 Perhaps this is Gregory v. Eads, 1 Vent. 27, 86 Eng. Rep. 20 (K.B. 1669).

17 Roe ex dem. Wilkinson v. Tranmer, 2 Wilson K.B. 75, 95 Eng. Rep. 694 (C.P. 1757). The other references to English authorities are not identifiable except for *Coke upon Littleton* and M. Bacon, *Abridgment*.

18 Hening's Statutes, vol. 5, p. 409.

at the legal exchange [with] the greater part in the paper emissions of July 1780, and the court ordered the suit to be dismissed, from which the plaintiffs appealed.

This cause was very fully argued and often upon general points, but [it] was adjudged on a circumstance peculiar to itself, which was this. The emissions of July 1780 were nominally at the rate of 40 for 1. They were paid into court on the 2d October and were expressly made a tender afterwards on the 16th October. The court delivered their opinions to the following effect.

Judge Mercer.

The question seems to be confined to the emissions of 14 July 1780. They, in my opinion, were issued for special purposes [and] were not payable generally in taxes but only in such as were imposed by that Act.[19] A very great proportion of the money paid being of this emission, the court erred in ordering it to be received and in dismissing the suit.

Anything made by the legislature [to be] money shall be a tender without any words particularly making it a tender. The clause of tender was introduced in some acts to save the debtor the hazard of keeping it, paying it into court at the time of plea and to stop interest, and not to make the emissions circulate as money.

The emissions of July 1780 came into circulation at the value of 40 for 1 and could be paid only at that ratio.

N.B. Mr. Mercer seemed to think that all emissions prior to the May Session of Assembly 1780 were after that to be tendered after the same rate of forty for one.

Judge Fleming.

I conceive the emissions of 14 July 1780 to have been distinct from all other emissions prior to them. They were current at the rate of forty for one and being receivable in

---

19  Hening's Statutes, vol. 10, pp. 248, 279, note also 321.

discharge of particular taxes, they were not to be tendered as money. Therefore [it was] error in the county court to receive it in the present case.

Judge Lyons.

Upon this appeal, two questions arise. First, whether any money emitted subsequent to the act of 1777[20] is to be considered as a legal tender. Secondly, whether the emissions of 14 July 1780 differ from other emissions of paper money in this respect.

As to the first question, an act of assembly is to be construed in a popular sense and not strictly according to grammar and therefore the monies emitted subsequent to 1777 are to be considered as a legal tender in some manner or other.

As to the second question, the emissions of 14 July 1780 were not applied to particular purposes but were [to be] made use of in every respect as other bills. There was a penalty for counterfeiting them.

Being of the value of forty for one, they were a tender at that rate, so that if enough had been paid into court, I should be for affirming what was done by the County Court, but enough not being paid their proceedings should be reversed for this error.

Chief Justice Carrington.

The emissions of 14 July 1780 were not a legal tender on the 2d day of October 1780 when they were paid into court. Let the judgment be reversed.

Query how far does the Act of 1781[21] affect this case inasmuch as thereby all payments are to be good for the nominal sum.

---

20 Hening's Statutes, vol. 9, pp. 287, 288, note also 297, 298.

21 Hening's Statutes, vol. 10, p. 398, note also 412, 456.

### Vaughan v. Moss

Appeal; Replevin Bond.

[There was a] judgment in the county court; fieri facias [was] executed and the effects replevied. Before the three months ran out, the judgment was reversed for error, but notwithstanding that when the three months ran out, [a] motion was made for judgment on the replevin bond, and judgment thereupon was given, from which an appeal was prayed to the General Court. Notwithstanding this appeal, the goods were executed [upon] a second time, and the debt [was] satisfied. 2 Strange 867.[22] 6 Mod. 23.

[The case was] adjourned for another argument.

### Stringer v. Stringer

Supersedeas.

The defendant was one of four justices who composed the court when issue was joined in the suit. [The judgment was] reversed for error.

April 1786

### Commonwealth v. Sorrel[23]

Indictment for murder.

A man sent for trial by a county court for manslaughter may be indicted for murder before the General Court. Three judges against two.

November 1787

### Reid and Ford v. Biddle etc.

Case of [a] foreign attachment in chancery.

---

22  Sweetapple v. Goodfellow, 2 Strange 867, 93 Eng. Rep. 903 (K.B 1763)

23  Also reported in 3 Va. (1 Va. Cas.) 253 (1786); Lee was counsel for the defendant.

1st. The assignment to the defendants does not comprehend the attached effects, and this being the ground on which the claim of the plaintiffs is opposed, there appears [to be] no obstacle to their demands. The assignment was fair and also the prior transfer of the goods which the defendants held as factors.

2d. Formerly citizens had a preference in attachments to foreigners and still will be preferred in all cases where they do not stand in an equal condition with foreigners in every point of advantage relative to the payment of their debts.

3d. This is the case of foreigners only, for the act done by Ford to acquire citizenship is considered by the court not as a reality but an appearance only.

4th. Risberg, who is plaintiff in another suit against the same effects commenced before they are ordered by this court to be applied to any particular debts, is in time and shall share in proportion with Reed and Ford.

5th. These debts being fully paid, the surplus may be distributed amongst the assignees and Tellier in proportion to the original stock of the parties.

6th. It remains to have it ascertained whether Richardson & Co. be connected with C. Biddle & Co. and Tellier.

Court of Appeals. November 1787

## Taylor v. Wallace[24]

Verbal gift accompanied with possession which remained four years is fraudulent and the title [is] defective.

General Court June 1789

[It was] ordered that the clerks of the said district courts do not docket any appeal received after the last day of the term to which the appeal is returnable without the leave of the court and that all appeals not docketed during the next suc-

---

24  Also reported in 8 Va. (4 Call) 92 (1786).

ceeding term shall stand dismissed and the clerks may grant certificates accordingly.

### Taylor's exrs. v. Taylor's exrs.

Adjudged by the Chancellor November 1789.

[The] act of limitation against a fraud unless the same is charged to have been discovered within the time of limitation is a good plea. 3 Wms. 143.

Equity regards length of time. 1 Ch. Rep. 139. 2 Ch. Rep. 48.

A suit is not pending till the bill be filed.

An appeal may be from an interlocutory decree though in this case the order is final. 3 Blackstone, *Commentaries*.

A man may demur ore tenus at the bar. 3 Wms. 371.[25]

March term 1791. High Court of Chancery.

### Hinde v. Pendleton[26]

[Auctions]

[It was] decreed upon the authority of a case reported in Cowper that at a sale by public auction, the person proposing to sell shall not buy by himself or another and therefore the bid of a by bidder for his use shall stand for nothing and the next bona fide bidder to him shall be considered as the purchaser and especially if his bid be equal to the reasonable value of the thing sold.

### Morgan v. Dorsey

An appeal.

Judgment was rendered on a motion against the sheriff charging him with a voluntary escape of a debtor, but the re-

---

25  South Sea Co. v. Wymondsell, 3 P. Wms. 143, 24 Eng. Rep. 1004 (Ch. 1732); Goddard v. Goddard, 1 Chan. Rep. 139, 21 Eng. Rep. 531 (Ch. 1639); Castlehaven v. Underhill, 2 Chan. Rep. 46, 21 Eng. Rep. 612 (Ch. 1670); W. Blackstone, *Commentaries*, vol. 3, p. 454 (1768); Tourton v. Flower, 3 P. Wms. 369, 24 Eng. Rep. 1105 (Ch. 1735).

26  Also reported in Wythe 354 (1791).

cord states no return of the sheriff that the prisoner was in custody in consequence of the warrant. Virginia Laws 304, 446.[27] [The judgment was] reversed.

### Cadwallader's exrs. v. Mason[28]

A question was made whether a devisee of mortgaged land be accountable to a mortgagee for the mesne profits.

To show he is not were cited. 3 Atkins 245, [and] 2 Atkins 120. A mortgagee is accountable for the mesne profits. Bunch v. Wright, reported in Dearnford and East.[29]

June 1791

### Champ's exrs. v. Starke[30]

Motion for a supersedeas before the [Court of] Appeals.

The action was brought since the act of frauds and perjuries[31] upon a verbal promise made prior thereto and a nonsuit was directed by the District Court of [    ] because the promise proved was only a verbal one and the action was commenced subsequent to the act of frauds. [The] motion [was] granted, the court saying that the point ought to be settled.

Also in this case it was determined that the executors need not give security for prosecuting the supersedeas because they were executors.

---

27  *Acts of Assembly Now in Force*, pp. 304, 446 (1769); reprinted in Hening's Statutes, vol. 6, pp. 344, 345, vol. 8, pp. 118, 119.

28  Also reported in Wythe 188 (1793).

29  Meade v. Lord Orrery, 3 Atk. 235, 26 Eng. Rep. 937 (Ch. 1745); French v. Baron, 2 Atk. 120, 26 Eng. Rep. 475 (Ch. 1740); Birch v. Wright, 1 Term Rep. 378, 99 Eng. Rep. 1148 (K.B. 1786).

30  Note the very similar case of Thornton, Exr. of Champ v. Jett, 1 Va. (1 Wash.) 138 (1792).

31  Act of Oct. 1785, c. 64, Hening's Statutes, vol. 12, pp. 160-162.

## Pollard v. Rogers[32]

Appeal from the Court of Chancery.

Rogers, the appellee, sold to the appellant a tract of land having then a good title only to a moiety, and subsequent to this sale [he] bought in a part of the outstanding titles to the other moiety. The bill was to set aside the contract, which was dismissed, and from the dismission, this appeal was made.

The decree was reversed as to that part of the tract of land to which the appellee had at the time of pronouncing the decree a good title and affirmed as to the rest of the cause.

The particular reasons that led to this decision are to me unknown.

## Downman v. Downman's exrs.[33]

An appeal.

The common bail entered himself as special bail and offered a plea of tender which did not state the sort of money nor the quantity of debt. The court refused the plea first because the plea was after [an] office judgment [and] secondly that the bills tendered as money were not current as money at the time of the tender.

Campbell for appellant contended that, after [an] office judgment a tender cannot be pleaded and cited 1 Burrow and Eq. Ca. Abr. Secondly [he said] that the court cannot notice the thing tendered because that was a subject fit for a jury. 5 Rep. 114.[34] A defendant is not bound to receive money tendered.

Curia. The Act of Assembly[35] allows only pleas to issue immediately. But this Act should be liberally construed and any

---

32  Also reported in 8 Va. (4 Call) 239 (1791).

33  Also reported in 1 Va. (1 Wash.) 26 (1791) and in Brown's reports, *infra*.

34  Wade's Case, 5 Co. Rep. 114, 77 Eng. Rep. 232 (C.P 1601).

35  Perhaps Act of Oct. 1787, c. 39, s. 20, Hening's Statutes, vol. 12, p. 544.

plea should be received which being put in issue will decide the cause according to its merit or justice. Where a bond has a collateral condition the plea of condition performed is usually allowed though it makes other pleadings necessary. A tender may be pleaded after imparlance. Str. 136, T. Raym. 254.[36]

But the judgment ought to be affirmed because the plea tendered was in itself bad.

1st. It was blank.

2dly. It states the principal sum and not the interest leaving that to future computation.

3d. The sort of money should be stated in the plea that it might be in the power of the plaintiff to demur to it if he pleased. Davis' *Reports*.[37] Money is a legal question determinable by a court, what it is, and not by a jury.

Whether the thing tendered as money should be current as such at the time of the plea is questionable but that in this case need not be decided.

[The] judgment [was] affirmed.

### Smith v. Harmanson[38]

Appeal from a district court.

An action of debt was brought in a county court upon a bond in the penalty of £2000 conditioned to pay £1000. The verdict was for £1147.8.4, and judgment was rendered for £2000 to be discharged by the payment of £1147.8.4 in the county court, from which there was an appeal to the district court, who reversed this judgment and entered another for £2000 to be discharged by the payment of £1000 and interest. The bond was not regularly made a part of the record.

---

36  Rochtschilt v. Leibman, 2 Strange 836, 93 Eng. Rep. 883 (K.B. 1729); Giles v. Hartis, 1 Ld. Raym. 254, 91 Eng. Rep. 1066 (K.B. 1697).

37  Case of Mixed Money, Davis 18 at 28, 80 Eng. Rep. 507 at 516 (P.C. 1604).

38  Also reported in 1 Va. (1 Wash.) 6 (1791) and in Brown's reports, *infra*.

This judgment, being variant from the verdict was held to be erroneous and for another reason, viz. because the bond was not a part of the record to which [the] judgment related. The first judgment was held to be erroneous also, but it being more in favor of the appellant, the court would not reverse it but affirmed it.

The court said the practice was right upon the Act of Assembly in not entering principal and interest as an aggregate sum and giving judgment for the same.

An adjudication similar to this was cited by Ronald.[39]

High Court of Chancery

### Morris v. Pickett[40]

The assignee of a bond for valuable consideration and [in] bona fide is not liable to any equity existing against the assignor of which he had not notice at the time of the assignment; but the court would enquire into the consideration paid, and, if it were not to the full value of the bond as to the difference the equity would be allowed as to that.

### Graham v. Graham

A trust deed prior to marriage and in consideration thereof is to be construed by the same rules of law as if the estate was a legal one, wherefore [it was] decided that the estate in this instance was an estate in special tail.

Fredericksburg District Court

### [In re Gray]

French Gray, as was supposed, committed suicide about two months ago. The coroner omitted to take an inquest upon the body as he might have done. The deceased made his will in which he devised a part of his personal property to a per-

39 Andrew Ronald; see Commonwealth v. Ronald, 8 Va. (4 Call) 97 (1786), where the lawyer was the defendant.
40 Affirmed, 2 Va. (2 Wash.) 255 (1796).

son not related to him nor entitled as a distributee of his estate in case he had died intestate.

At the instance of one of the distributees, an inquisition was presented to the grand jury stating French Gray to have been felo de se. Though no precedent from the English books was produced, the court suffered the grand jury to take the inquisition and to examine witnesses touching the same, who returned it to be a true bill, and the same was received by the court.

### Winslow v. Stockdell

An action of trespass for mesne profits.

Plaintiff was heir in tail, whose father devised the land to and died, who entered and sold the same to the defendant, who possessed the same for twenty-two years ago, and by a decree in chancery the plaintiff recovered the land. The time of the trespasses was prior to any actual possession as found in the special verdict. The defendant rests the cause upon this question, whether the plaintiff could recover for a trespass prior to his first actual possession and [he] cited Co. Rep., Liffard's Case; 2 Barnes 367, Stanyhout v. [    ];[41] Co. Lit. 142. The ad quod damnum was executed under the former Act of Assembly prior to 1748.[42] Judgment [was given] for the defendant.

### Pendleton v. Carter

In debt.

This suit was founded on a promissory note for the payment of a sum of money with interest from the date. The verdict was for the debt in the declaration mentioned to be discharged by the payment of the sum due with interest from the 1st November 1769 till paid. It was moved in arrest of judgment that, in debt without a penalty, a verdict and judg-

---

41 Liford's Case, 11 Co. Rep. 46, 77 Eng. Rep. 1206 (K.B. 1614); Stanynought v. Cosins, Barnes 457, 94 Eng. Rep. 1002 (C.P. 1746).

42 *Cf.* Act of Oct. 1748, c. 1, s. 16, Hening's Statutes, vol. 5, p. 414.

ment cannot be rendered so as to carry interest subsequent to the judgment, but this objection was overruled.

### Boyer v. M'Clenachan

A wife is entitled to dower in a trust estate in this country, the reason for the contrary doctrine in England not prevailing here.

### Heathcote & Fenwick v. Martin

If British creditors and the assignees of a bankrupt, according to the British laws, were pursuing the effects of the debtor here, the assignees should be preferred and the bill of the former dismissed. But if the competition was between an American citizen creditor and the assignees of a British subject bankrupt concerning his effects and credits, the American creditor should be preferred unless the assignees would bring into a dividend all the assets in that as well as this country, in which latter case all the bankrupt's creditors would be placed upon an equal footing without respect to their country, nor would this court compel the American creditor to seek redress in Great Britain.

### Anonymous

[It is] improper for this court to direct any testimony to be admitted upon a trial at law because it is possible that, at the trial, a witness who may have been examined in this court may be proved to have been incompetent and if so the deposition ought not to be read. Depositions regularly taken here may be read at the trial at law unless incompetency be proved at the time it was sworn to.

### Alexander v. Murray

It is a rule of equity that a vendee upon giving up his deposit as well as all rights to the thing bought may be discharged. 1 Wms. 745, Saville v. Saville.[43]

---

43   Savile v. Savile, 1 P. Wms. 745, 24 Eng. Rep. 596 (Ch. 1721).

### Roush v. Carver

An appeal from a decree in a county court.

Carver brought his bill for a conveyance of a title under a patent which Roush had obtained bearing date prior to a patent for the same land to Carver and obtained a decree.

One Cheifly had made an entry and obtained a warrant from the office of Lord Fairfax in the year [    ][44], which by sundry sales became vested in Roush, for a tract of land containing 400 acres adjoining a tract of Lord Fairfax. He and Roush obtained a patent for it. Many years previous to this entry, Lord Fairfax had made a survey for a tract containing near 700 acres in which it appears the 400 acres was a part, and these 700 acres he leased for a term of years. Carver made an entry with Lord Fairfax in his office for the 700 acres, but his patent was obtained subsequent to that of Roush, and Lord Fairfax conveyed his right in the lease. One principal question was made.

First. Whether the 400 acres were not to be considered as waste and ungranted, notwithstanding Lord Fairfax's survey, it not being made an entry and warrant recorded in the public book of his office but only recorded in his book of private estate. [It was] determined [that] this was not necessary, and the reason urged, that this was necessary in order to give notice to Chiefly was deemed insufficient especially as notice appears to have been had from the terms of Chiefly's entry.

Second. Lord Fairfax [was] a private man as to his estate and might reserve for his own use a part of his lands notwithstanding his public invitation to settlers and the method he took [was] sufficient in the present case inasmuch as Chiefly appears by his entry [    ]lt had notice of the reservation. [The] decree [was] affirmed.

---

44  Date left blank in the manuscript.

## Proudfit v. Blane[45]

[There was a] decree against [the] defendant as an absentee about two years ago. At this term, a motion was made to re-docket it and for leave to file the answer and to try it on the merits. After argument of the 39th Section,[46] the motion was granted etc.

Federal court.

## Harwood v. Lewis[47]

Debt on bond conditioned for the payment of certificates.

[The] jury estimated the damages by the value of certificates when their verdict was rendered. [There was] a motion for a new trial on the ground of excessive damages, the rule that the jury ought to have adopted being the value when the contract was broken. [The] authorities cited [were] Dutch v. Warren in Strange, Powell on *Contracts* 137, Graves v. Groves in the Court of Appeals.[48] [A] new trial [was] denied, the court saying that notwithstanding the precedents, the rule adopted by the jury was the just one.

## Curry v. Burns[49]

An appeal from a decree of Berkeley County.

Burns made a survey in the year 1757 but failed to apply for a grant within the time limited by the rules of Lord Fairfax's office. Another person thereafter applied for a part of the same land in the year 1768 and, complying in all respects with the rules of the office, obtained a grant, which has been conveyed regularly to Curry. This grant recites the forfeited

---

45 Same case on appeal: 7 Va. (3 Call) 207 (1802).

46 Perhaps Act of Oct. 1792, c. 12, s. 39, Hening's Statutes, vol. 13, p. 418.

47 Reversed 10 U.S. (6 Cranch) 82 (1810).

48 Dutch v. Warren, 1 Strange 406, 93 Eng. Rep. 598 (1720); Groves v. Graves, 1 Va. (1 Wash.) 1 (1790).

49 Also reported in 2 Va. (2 Wash.) 121 (1795); Lee was counsel for the appellant; note also the further litigation in 7 Va. (3 Call) 183 (1802).

right of Burns. Curry recovered the land in ejectment which Burns enjoined in the County Court of Berkeley, and the injunction was there made perpetual. This suit was commenced in 1785. From this decree, Curry appealed, and the court affirmed the decree whereby the injunction was ordered to be perpetual, and Curry [was] ordered to convey his title to Burns.

The court said [that] without the Act of 1786[50], which was made to procure and substantiate such rights as that of Burns, he had an equitable right to the land in question. This Act might and did corroborate the rights. In this case Burns having obtained a patent in the year 1788 according to law, though junior to the patent under which Curry claims, yet by relation, it shall go back to the equitable right and prevail at law over the older patent. This was laid down in another case which was carried to the Court of Appeals, and what was there done this court does not recollect. So that a conveyance from Curry is unnecessary but does not vitiate the decree.

Mr. Williams said that the [Court of] Appeals had confirmed the doctrine in the case of Maese against Hambleton.[51]

A divided court.

## Wilson v. Rucker[52]

A military certificate [that was] lost may be recovered from the bona fide purchaser for valuable consideration. The case of lost money or notes [is] not alike [as] determined by the Court of Chancery.

---

50  Hening's Statutes, vol. 12, pp. 237-240.

51  Maze v. Hamilton, 8 Va. (4 Call) 33 (1783); note also the connected cases in Wythe 51 (1789) and 8 Va. (4 Call) 196 (1791).

52  Also reported in Wythe 296 (1794) and reversed on other grounds in 5 Va. (1 Call) 500 (1799).

# Turner v. Stip[53]

An appeal to the Court of Appeals.

By the Act of 1748,[54] a deed is good between the parties though never recorded and the execution of the deed may be proved before a jury, as any other fact by one witness. Refusing this testimony was error in the county court, and their judgment was for this properly reversed by the district court, whose judgment is affirmed here.

---

[53] Also reported in 1 Va. (1 Wash.) 319 (1794); Lee was counsel for the appellant.

[54] Hening's Statutes, vol. 5, p. 410.

# JOHN BROWN

John Brown was born on October 4, 1750, in Williamsburg, Virginia. He learned the skills of a court clerk as an apprentice in the office of Benjamin Waller, the clerk of the colonial General Court of Virginia. He was appointed clerk of the court of Mecklenburg County and was sworn into office on July 10, 1775. According to Frederick Johnston, "from the records left in his office, he was a good clerk, and everything [was] kept in good order." In 1781 Brown was appointed clerk of the General Court of Virginia which required him to move to Richmond. Therefore, he appointed William Baskervill on June 4, 1781, to act as his deputy. He held the clerkship of Mecklenburg County until February 9, 1795, when he resigned to be succeeded by Baskervill.[1] He held the clerkship of the General Court until 1794. He made a collection of reports of General Court cases, but unfortunately they have been lost.[2]

In addition, he was clerk of the Court of Appeals, the highest court of Virginia, from 1785 until his death in 1810. Apparently, the Virginia appellate courts were not very busy before 1795, for Brown was also the clerk of the District Court of Richmond during the period 1789 to 1793 and clerk of the Court of Chancery in 1787. It is easy to see why he was interested in the law of court costs, which was so often the focus of his reports.[3]

---

1  Bruton and Middleton Parish Register 1662-1797, Photostat in the Virginia State Library, f. 10; *Virginia Gazette,* 26 March 1772; L. G. Tyler, "Abstracts of Marriage License Bonds" *Wm. & Mary Q.,* 1st ser., vol. 1, p. 49 (1892); *Mecklenburg County Order Books,* No. 4 (1773-1779), p. 314, No. 5 (1779-1784), p. 97, No. 8 (1792-1795), p. 391; S. N. Hurst and R. M. Brown, *Digest* (1897), vol. 1, p. 22; F. Johnston, *Memorials of Old Virginia Clerks* (1888), p. 245; P.H. Baskervill, *Genealogy of the Baskerville Family* (1912), p. 63; W. H. Bryson, "John Brown" in *Virginia Law Reporters Before 1880* (1977), pp. 87-89.

2  These reports were known to Conway Robinson; see above.

3  W.T. Hutchinson, W. M. E. Rachal, *Papers of James Madison,* vol. 4, p. 209, n. 5 (1965); *Calendar of Virginia State Papers* vols. 3-9 *passim* (1883-1890); Treasurer's Office Receipt Books, *passim,* in the Virginia State Library.

Brown acted as clerk of the Court of Appeals until his death in Richmond on October 31, 1810. He was characterized in the *Virginia Patriot* shortly after his death as "long well known for his superior talents in the line of his profession, and highly esteemed for his urbanity of manners and general good deportment."

## BROWN'S REPORTS

The original manuscript of John Brown's reports of Virginia cases in the Court of Appeals from 1791 to 1799 is in the Virginia State Library.[4] This heretofore unidentified manuscript of reports of cases in the Court of Appeals is remarkable in that the reporter was so concerned with clerical details and points of appellate procedure to the frequent neglect of the substantive law. The comparison of the handwriting of this manuscript and that of the clerk of the Court of Appeals at the time of these reports shows that these reports were made by John Brown.[5]

Brown's reports cover the period 1791 to 1799. These reports were continued in a second booklet which is now lost; on the front cover of this manuscript is written "No. 1" and "See page 18th, 2 Book, for entries of some notes of decisions prior to 1791--omitted to be entered first, the rough notes being mislaid." The lost reports of General Court cases that Conway Robinson cited appears to be a third volume; Robinson cited six cases dating from 1788 to 1794.[6]

In transcribing these reports, italics have been used for comments which seem to have been added by another hand at a later time. References to the reports of Bushrod Washington and Daniel Call were added to these manuscripts by William Green, the legal scholar who died in 1880, but these are

---

4    MS. 21779c2.; I would like to thank the Virginia State Librarian for permission to publish this manuscript.

5    This identification was corroborated by the opinions of Charles T. Cullen, William Ray, and E. Lee Shepard, who very kindly came to my assistance.

6    See above.

omitted because this information has been included in the footnotes.

Brown's reports were first published in the *University of Richmond Law Review,* volume 11, pages 711-741 (1977).

### Ellis v. McCall

June 7th 1791. The Court overruled the motion for a writ of [   ] on the merits and, after some conversation on the necessity of making an entry of the motion and decision, directed it to be made, although the parties wished it not to be done.

### Thweat v. Finch[7]

[Revivor by appellee]

June 7th 1791. The appellant being dead, his executor wished the appeal to abate, but the court determined that the appellee, without the consent of the executor, might revive[8] it by scire facias which was accordingly awarded. They also said that it was at the appellee's option either to permit an appeal to be dismissed, if not prosecuted, or to open the record for the decision of the court upon the regularity of the proceedings.

### Downman v. Downman's Exors.[9]

June 10th 1791. [There was an] appeal from an office judgment in [the] district court which the appellant offered to set aside on the third day of the district court by filing a plea of tender, which plea was refused. The court here said that any plea after [an] office judgment by which, when an issue at law or in fact is made up, an end will be wholly put to the dispute ought to be received, but this plea *of tender* the court below were right to refuse, for the second reason assigned by

---

7   Further proceedings in this case are reported in 1 Va. (1 Wash.) 217 (1793); note also the connected case of Thweatt v. Jones, 22 Va. (1 Rand.) 328 (1823).

8   receive *MS.*

9   Also reported in 1 Va. (1 Wash.) 26 (1791) and Lee's reports, *supra;* note also the further comment which follows the next case.

them *to wit because the money brought into Court is what was once paper money but is not now in April 1790 money under any des[ ]. See [the] reason (as entered in order book) in next page.* [The] judgment [was] affirmed.

See Wash. Rep., vol. 1, p. 26.

### Smith v. Harmanson[10]

[There was an] appeal to [the] Accomack District Court from a judgment in [the] Northampton County Court for £2000 and costs to be discharged [by] £1147.18.1 and costs, which is the sum found by the jury [to be] owing and is supposed to contain the aggregate sum of principal and interest to the day of judgment. This judgment was reversed by the District Court for that reason, and they gave judgment for £2000 to be discharged by £1000 with interest from 21st April 1783 till payment. From this judgment, the debtor having become insolvent, Smith, the creditor appeals. The court here said that, upon reversing the judgment, the District Court ought either to have directed a new trial to ascertain the debt, or, as the error was in favor of the debtor and not complained of by the creditor, the judgment of the County Court ought to have been affirmed. [The] judgment of [the] District Court [was] reversed, and [the] judgment of [the] County Court [was] affirmed with damages from the day of the judgment in the County Court to the time of [the] reversal in the District Court. A copy of the bond, of which oyer was not prayed, was added by the clerk to the record, but the court's observation on it I could not hear.

### Downman v. Downman's Exors.

When about to enter the judgment, the judge presiding in court, upon being asked, said that when the court wished a reason for their judgment to be entered on [the] record they would direct it to be done. *But in this case, though an affirmance, the court at the reading of the orders had this reason, "The court*

10  Also reported in 1 Va. (1 Wash.) 6 (1791) and Lee's reports, *supra.*

*having properly refused the plea upon the second reason" interlined after the words "no error in the said judgment."*

## Dade et al. v. Alexander[11]

[Interest and Costs]

June 17th 1791. This court having considered all the ca[ses] respecting damages on affirming chancery decrees wa[s of the] opinion that no damages, however justly entitled [thereto] the appellees might in such cases be, were given [ ] and directed the decree to be affirmed with costs only.

## Pleasants v. Bibbs[12]

Three appeals.

In these cases, the direction of the General Court in *Cosby v. Stodghill* was confirmed. *i.e. that bonds for paper money ought to be sealed according to the time mentioned in the condition for carrying interest if that time should be antecedent to the date of the bond.*

## Armistead v. Jordan

[A] judgment in [the] County Court on [a] replevin bond entered into not for the penalty but [for] the sum due with interest [was] affirmed in [the] District Court. And upon appeal to this court the judgment of the District Court was affirmed, no other error being alleged.

## Keel etc. v. Herbert[13]

The court in this case, the record (except the one filed with the petition which the court did not consider as the record) not being returned, directed the clerk to award a writ of certiorari to the judges of the District Court to certify the record fully and also to issue the like writ whenever a writ of super-

---

11  Also reported in 1 Va. (1 Wash.) 30 (1791).

12  Also reported in 1 Va. (1 Wash.) 8 (1791).

13  Further proceedings in this case are reported in 1 Va. (1 Wash.) 138, 203 (1792, 1793) and *infra*.

sedeas was first awarded either out of term or in term and to consider these directions as general.

### Henderson etc. v. Southall and DuVal[14]

One of the appellees being dead, the court, being informed thereof, directed an abatement to be entered as to him and judgment to be entered for [the] surviving appellees.

### Singleton v. Madison

Common law appeal from Kentucky.

On a doubt of the clerk, the court directed judgment to be entered for damages on the affirmance.

### Hambleton et al. v. Wells[15]

[Mistake of clerk is not error as to defendants]

An appeal from a judgment in ejectment versus the appellants for the lands claimed by the appellee, the defendants were made at three different times, an issue for the whole lands was made up as to two of them, but the other was made a defendant only and put in no plea, which was alleged to be error. But the court considered the want of a plea as to this defendant as a misprision of the clerk and of no consequence as the defendants as to whom issue was joined defended for the whole land. But [the] judgment was reversed for another reason, which is entered on record.

### Hudson v. Johnson[16]

[Costs]

An action for debt [was] brought by the appellant in the County Court, which appears, by a demurrer to the evidence, to have been paid after the bringing of the suit. The County

---

14  Earlier proceedings in this case are reported in 8 Va. (4 Call) 371 (1790).

15  Also reported in 8 Va. (4 Call) 213 (1791) and in 11 Va. (1 Hen. & M.) 307 n. (1791).

16  Also reported in 1 Va. (1 Wash.) 10 (1791).

Court overruled the demurrer and gave judgment for the appellee for full costs. On an appeal to the District Court, so much of the judgment as gave the costs preceding the payment was reversed; but notwithstanding that, damages on the affirmance as to the residue were awarded the appellee, from which the appellant appealed to this court. The court here said that a payment made after the bringing of the suit was equal to bringing the money into court and that the suit ought to have been dismissed at the defendant's costs but that the judgment of the District Court as to the damages awarded was erroneous. And therefore it was reversed as to those damages and affirmed as to the residue.

### Browne v. Belscher[17]

[Arbitration waived by consent]

After the suit in the court below had been referred to arbitration, the parties went on to trial of the issue by a jury without setting aside the order of reference. And this court being of opinion that the proceeding to trial in such case by consent was not [an] erroneous proceeding, affirmed the judgment of the District Court, which affirmed the judgment given below for the plaintiff in the original action.

### Croughton v. Peachy et al.

November 22nd 1791. Judgment was obtained in the district court against three defendants, but only Croughton prayed an appeal. The court, being applied to, said that the judgment was to be affirmed as to all three but the damages and costs paid by the one appealing only, and that he alone was to be entered as appellant, but in the recital it must be shown that the judgment in the district court was against the other two also. But it being said that Mr. Brooke was concerned for the appellant who did not appear, judgment was directed for that reason only not to be entered.

---

17 Also reported in 1 Va. (1 Wash.) 9 (1791).

## Woodson etc., exors. of Benjamin Woodson, exor. of John Woodson, exor. of Booth Woodson v. William Fitzpatrick

[liability of executor]

[There was a] motion for a supersedeas to a judgment of the District Court of Charlottesville affirming a judgment of [the] Fluvanna [County] Court entered "To be levied of the effects of Benjamin Woodson (who by his assumpsit for his testator had made himself liable) if sufficient but if not the costs to be levied of the executor's goods." The reason alleged for the supersedeas was that the judgment which made the executor's own estate liable as above ought to have been entered "To be levied of the effects of Booth Woodson if sufficient, but if not then of the effects of Benjamin." But the court overruled the motion and said that, where a suit was brought against an executor who had made the testator's debt his own by his assumpsit the judgment ought to be absolute against the executor although he may be styled executor in the proceedings which in such case there is no necessity for doing, but where an executor is sued for a debt of his testator and he must of necessity be sued as executor, if he by his false pleading makes himself liable, then the judgment must be entered for debt etc. "To be levied of the testator's effects if sufficient but if not of the executor's own effects." Query?

## Jones etc. v. Logwood[18]

[Scroll as seal]

The court among other things in this cause determined that a scroll used as a seal and acknowledged as such prior to the passage of the Act in 1788[19] on that subject was a good seal.

---

18  Also reported in 1 Va. (1 Wash.) 42 (1791).

19  Hening's Statutes, vol. 12, p. 749.

April Term 1792

When an appeal or other cause is dismissed for want of appearance, the default is to be entered of the party or parties failing to appear. See *Standfin v. Hunt*, page 147.

Appeals coming to the clerk on or before the end of the second term [are] to be docketed by him without inquiring by whom they were brought.

### Charles Hudson, exor. of Christopher Hudson v. Ross etc.[20]

[Executor not personally liable for interest and costs]

Judgment [was] entered against Christopher Hudson in [the] Amelia [County] Court, from which he appealed, and pending the appeal, he died. And on the motion of [the] present appellant, a scire facias was awarded him as executor of the said Christopher to revive and hear errors, which writ the appellant did not prosecute. Afterwards a scire facias was awarded [to] the appellees which was returned executed on the executor now appellant by which the court here said he was become a party. The judgment of the county court was affirmed by the district court with damages as if all the parties to the county court's judgment had been living, and from this judgment the executor appealed to this court. Upon deliberation, the court here determined that the district court's judgment was erroneous in not awarding the damages and costs upon the affirmance against the testator's estate in the hands of his executor who had been brought into court by the scire facias and made a party and that the case of *Gordon v. Bates*[21] in this court, which subjects the executor's own estate in case of a deficiency of assets to the payment of the damages and costs, was in that respect a wrong decision which was not particularly attended to because of the smallness of

---

20  Also reported in 1 Va. (1 Wash.) 74 (1792).
21  Bates v. Gordon, 7 Va. (3 Call) 555 (1790).

the sum on which the damages on the affirmance were to run.

[The] judgment of [the] district court [was] reversed with costs. [The] judgment of [the] county court [was] affirmed with damages and costs to be levied of the testator's estate only in his executor's hands. The court also said that it was probable [that] the judgment of the district court would have been right in not taking notice of the executor if he had not been before the court by the scire facias.

### Bibb etc. v. Commonwealth[22]

[Suit on a sheriff's bond]

This suit was prosecuted in the district court in the name of *"the Commonwealth for the benefit of Catharine Cawthorne"* upon a sheriff's bond dated in 1787 for performance of his office made payable to the Commonwealth in the penalty of £1000, and judgment was entered "that the *Commonwealth* recover against the *defendants for the benefit of* C. C. £1000" and costs but to be "discharged by the payment of the damages aforesaid and such other damages as may be hereafter assessed upon suing out a scire facias and assigning new breaches." [An] objection [was made] by [the] appellants that the bond ought to have been taken to the justices pursuant to the Ordinance of Convention in 1776[23] and not to the Commonwealth.

[It was held] by the court [that] this Ordinance is temporary in its nature and does not repeal the act in 1748[24] which was amended by an Act in 1753[25] directing the penalty of £1000 payable to the *King* and giving the same remedy to the party injured as is given by the Ordinance and the legislature considered the law of 1748 as in force in 1782 referring to it at

22  Also reported in 1 Va. (1 Wash.) 91 (1792).

23  Hening's Statutes, vol. 9, p. 128.

24  Hening's Statutes, vol. 5, p. 516.

25  Hening's Statutes, vol. 6, p. 344.

that time and changing the mode,[26] and this bond of Bibb's pursuing the form of those laws substituting the Commonwealth for the King is right upon the merits, but the judgment "attaching the recovery to C. Cawthorne as to future injuries excluding all others" is erroneous. [They] reversed, and judgment [was] entered for [the] Commonwealth for £1000 debt and costs to be discharged "by the payment of £162 the damages assessed *for the benefit of the said C. C.* and the costs and such other damages as may be hereafter assessed *upon a scire facias being sued out thereon and new breaches assigned by the said C. or any other person or persons injured.*"

The words [in bold italic type] were added, and those [in just italic type] were entered by the direction of the court, the rule formerly entered being adjudged to confine the remedy for future injuries to the said C. C. only.

### Taylor v. Dundass[27]

[Execution is valid until quashed]

A judgment was obtained in [the] Fairfax [County] Court by Dundass against Hendricks and Taylor, upon which an execution against the goods issued and was served on those of Hendricks only, who gave a twelve month's bond with security. Afterwards, another fieri facias issued and was served on Taylor's property, who moved the Court of Fairfax to quash the last execution, which was done accordingly. To this judgment quashing the second execution, a supersedeas issued out of [the] Dumfries District Court, where the said judgment was reversed, and from the judgment of the District Court, Taylor appealed to this court.

The court here was of opinion that the judgment of the District Court was erroneous "the evidence offered by the appellee tending to prove that the first execution was issued and

---

26  Hening's Statutes, vol. 11, p. 168.

27  Also reported in 1 Va. (1 Wash.) 92 (1792); later proceedings are reported *sub nom.* Hendricks v. Dundass, *infra* and in 2 Va. (2 Wash.) 50 (1795).

executed improperly although if true [it were] a good ground for quashing the first execution if the appellee had made a motion for that purpose did not apply in opposition to the quashing of the second execution which issued after the first as returned executed and remained in that state this court being of opinion that under the Act of Assembly[28] a bond to replevy, whilst the execution remains unquashed is as much a complete execution of the judgment as if the estate had been sold to the full amount of the debt and the party is left to pursue his new remedy on that bond." [The] judgment of [the] District Court [was] reversed, and [the] judgment of [the] County Court [was] affirmed.

The president, in giving [the] opinion, said "that after a fieri facias had been once served" and returned executed "a new execution could not issue whatever has become of the estate until the execution so served is quashed."

It appears by the bill of exceptions that the appellee offered to prove by less than a record that the first execution issued without the order or direction of himself or his attorney; he also offered proof to show that Taylor undertook the management of the first execution and that the same under the care and management of the said Taylor's agent was unduly served and unfairly executed, but the County Court refused to admit the proof.

[general rule]

The court directed an entry to be made of the argument of a cause or of a continuance of the argument from day to day whether any other entry was made in any other case or not.

## Verell v. Coleman[29]

[Default judgment]

Coleman sued Verell in the County Court of Dinwiddie and after the suit was at issue, Verell was delivered up by his

---

28   Hening's Statutes, vol. 12, pp. 458, 459.

29   Also reported in 8 Va. (4 Call) 230 (1793).

special bail, and [he] obtained a writ of habeas corpus from the superior court, upon which the sheriff returned the cause of detention. Coleman filed a new declaration in the district court and took a common order which was confirmed, and judgment became final for want of the appearance of Verell; after the confirmation of the common order, a copy of the proceedings of the county court was filed with the district clerk; to this judgment a supersedeas was awarded.

The court here was of opinion that the habeas corpus suspended the proceedings in the court below; that the proceedings in the court above may be de novo or a certiorari may be awarded to bring up the record; that as the said Verell, the defendant below, moved the suit, it was his business to have attended to it, and, not having done so, he must submit to the consequences. And therefore the proceedings de novo in the district court being right and [there being] no error in the judgment by default, the same was affirmed.

## Hubbard v. Blow etc.[30]

[Recovery limited by pleadings]

[In an] original suit brought on a note of hand for £319.8.7 with interest, the declaration stated the sum right but omitted that part of the note relating to interest. The defendant without oyer pleaded payment and afterwards withdrew his plea and suffered judgment by non sum informatus, which was entered for principal with interest as expressed in the note and then appealed to the District Court of Prince Edward, in which court, the County Court's judgment was affirmed. Upon the appeal to the Court of Appeals, both judgments were reversed, and judgment [was] entered according to the demand in the declaration without interest.

---

[30]  Also reported in 1 Va. (1 Wash.) 70 (1792) and in 8 Va. (4 Call) 224 (1792).

## William Thompson v. Davenport[31]

One David Davenport was a defendant below with the appellant Thompson but did not join in the prayer for appeal, the clerk, on recording the order made on the hearing, applied to the court to know whether said D. Davenport's name should be inserted as party appellant or not and the court directed his name to be omitted as he did not appeal nor bring his case before them. October 16th 1792.

## Ross etc. v. Poythress[32]

An appeal from a judgment of [the] Petersburg District Court given for the appellee in a suit brought by the appellants against the appellee upon a prison bounds bond on the following verdict "We find for the plaintiffs and do assess their damages to £736.16.8, but if in the opinion of the court, a subpoena of injunction issued from the High Court of Chancery and delivered to the sheriff having the defendant Lacey in custody and served on the plaintiffs' attorney whereby the judgment on which the defendant was confined was enjoined was a sufficient authority to the sheriff to discharge him from custody under that execution, then we find for the defendant."

The court being unanimously of opinion that an injunction after a capias ad satisfaciendum executed does discharge the body out of custody affirmed the judgment of the District Court. The court *seemed* to think in this case that the security for the bounds could not be responsible as it appears by the jury's finding that the defendant was discharged by the sheriff, who, if he had not been justified by the injunction would have been liable for a voluntary escape.

---

31  Also reported in 1 Va. (1 Wash.) 125 (1792).

32  Also reported in 1 Va. (1 Wash.) 120 (1792).

## Redford v. Wiseman

A new appeal to this term.

The appellee this day made application to the court to affirm the judgment alleging as the only cause for trying the appeal at the first term that the appeal was merely for [the] sake of delay and that he had given notice, which was produced with an affidavit thereto that he would this day move this court for an affirmance. But the court refused to take the cause up at this term because it was not one of those causes which, from the nature or circumstances of them, required a speedy decision as for instance concerning a will or mill or similar to *Groves v. Graves*,[33] where the appellee was in confinement under a judgment, the propriety of which was disputed on the appeal.

## Keel etc. v. Herbert's exor.[34]

In the lifetime of Herbert, the plaintiffs sued out their writ of supersedeas, which, after it went from the office, had the word "Executor" interlined after the word Herbert, to whom notice was to be given, but by whom or whether before or after the service of was not known. At the last term, the circumstances above being made known on the motion of the plaintiffs, a new writ of supersedeas was awarded against the executor of the defendant in the first writ as a continuing process. But the court, having now considered the propriety of issuing a new writ, quashed it as being improper and awarded a scire facias to hear error as a proper writ.

### Bird v. Wallace, Johnson, and Muier

[There was an] appeal from a judgment affirming a judgment rendered on an assumpsit for sterling money damages.

---

[33] 1 Va. (1 Wash.) 1 (1790).

[34] Earlier proceedings in this case are reported *supra*; this stage is also reported in 1 Va. (1 Wash.) 138 (1792); later proceedings are reported in 1 Va. (1 Wash.) 203 (1793) and *infra*.

The appellant's attorney acknowledged there was no error, but, after the judgment of affirmance here was entered, he supposed that the damages ought to have been in current money and applied to the court for their opinion on that point. They said that, as the account arose on a sterling money contract, the judgment was right and that the damages in actions on the case ought to be laid in sterling money if the contract was payable in it.

### Thompson et al., exors. v. Jett[35]

Upon the quashing of this supersedeas because the plaintiffs had abandoned their suit by submitting to the nonsuit in the district court, the court awarded costs against them on a motion for that purpose as they were suing in the original suit on an assumpsit made to themselves, they directed in this case that no certificate should be made of record to the district court.

*See Carr, exor. of Carr v. Anderson, April 1808.*[36] *The question whether an absolute judgment for costs or one against [the] testator's goods if sufficient if not was settled by the court after consideration.*

April term 1793

### Keel etc. v. Herbert[37]

April Court 1793. The damages assessed being larger than those laid in the declaration the defendant acknowledged error, and [the] judgment [was] reversed, and the court then directed the verdict to be set aside and the cause sent back and referred to, to reverse the proceedings in toto. *The true name of the case is Blodget v. Brown et al.12 April 1793.*[38]

---

35 Also reported *sub nom.* Champ v. Jett, 1 Va. (1 Wash.) 138 (1792); further proceedings are reported *infra sub nom.* Thornton v. Jett (1793).

36 12 Va. (2 hen. & M.) 361 at 369, 370 (1808), which quotes from the record of Thornton v. Jett, *infra.*

37 Also reported in 1 Va. (1 Wash.) 203 (1793); earlier proceedings are reported *supra* and in 1 Va. (1 Wash.) 138 (1792); later proceedings are reported *infra.*

### McGuire v. Parker's exors.

An appeal [was] granted at the chancery term in September 1792 on [a] bond being given by the first day of the then next chancery term, which sat on the 1st day of March last. The court directed this cause to be put on the docket as a new one to this term considering the last October term, which intervened between the granting [of] the appeal and [the] giving [of the] bond, not as the term to which the appeal was granted.

### Daniel v. Robinson, exor. of Robinson[39]

[Revival of appeal by appellee]

The appellee being deceased her executors came into court and moved the court that the appeal might be revived in their names against the appellants who made default. And the cause now heard, it was suggested that a writ of scire facias ought to issue to warn the appellants. But the court said that the appeal might be revived without [it] and heard immediately it being the business of the appellants to follow their cause. [The] judgment [was] affirmed.

### Garland v. Atkinson

[Record on appeal]

April 12th 1793. On opening the record in this cause, the appellee's counsel discovered that the forthcoming bond was not in the record and applied to the court to know whether it was necessary or not. And two of the judges being of different opinions, the president thought it would be the better way to take out a certiorari to certify the diminution. But the court afterwards said that the appellee might without a certiorari get a fuller record from the clerk and file in lieu of the present one, which advice was pursued and the cause [was] left open for such record to be produced.

38 This last comment was written by William Green.
39 Also reported in 1 Va. (1 Wash.) 154 (1793).

N.B. the appellants made default.

## White v. Johnson[40]

[Failure to require bail; deputy sheriffs]

Johnson brought a suit in the General Court against one Watson and put the writ without directing it to the sheriff into the hands of the plaintiff, White, who served it on Watson without taking bail and returned it executed adding to the end of his name the letters "DS"[41] omitting the name of his principal. The defendant Watson failing to appear, a cognovit was entered and afterwards affirmed against him and the plaintiff White as deputy sheriff of [      ][42] County. Upon the execution of the writ of inquiry judgment was entered against Watson and [the] said White as deputy sheriff of *Louisa* County, to this judgment White obtained a supersedeas and objected among other things that there was no law authorizing a judgment in such case against a deputy sheriff. The court said that by an Act[43] passed in 1763 (until which time the deputy sheriffs here were in the same situation with those in England), a remedy was first given by motion [for judgment] against a deputy sheriff for money received by execution only in the first instance in favor of the creditor, or if he proceeded against the high sheriff, then in the second instance, to such high sheriff, and by the same law, the deputy sheriff was directed to put his own name as well as that of his principal to all mesne process executed by him, but if he failed to do so, that there was no law authorizing a judgment on such mesne process against him. They said [that] the practice in the General Court before [the] war and since was to proceed in such cases against the deputy sheriff but that such practice was not warranted by any law. And therefore the judgment and all the proceedings subsequent to the declara-

---

40  Also reported in 1 Va. (1 Wash.) 159 (1793).

41  I. e. deputy sheriff.

42  Left blank in the manuscript.

43  Hening's Statutes, vol. 7, pp. 648-649.

tion were set aside, and the cause [was] sent back to the General Court to be proceeded in anew on the sheriff's return.

After the rising of the court this day, Mr. Pendleton, being asked, told me that the proceedings were to be carried on hereafter against the defendant and [the] high sheriff, whose name the party was to let me know, and not against the deputy as the sheriff and that the court thought that the writ, notwithstanding [that] it was not directed, was properly and regularly served.

### Banister's exors. v. Shore's admr.[44]

[Costs in equity]

This suit was brought by the appellee as administrator of his wife, the daughter of the appellant's testator, for the recovery of the alleged marriage portion of the daughter, for which a decree was obtained in the court of chancery; but upon an appeal to this court the decree was reversed, and the bill [was] dismissed but without costs either on the reversal or dismissal by the particular direction of the court, who said that no costs ought to be paid by the appellee as the suit was brought for the recovery of a claim supposed to be due to the intestate.

### Reynolds v. Walter's admr.[45]

[It was] directed by the president that no costs on the reversal be awarded against the appellee for [the] reason mentioned in the above note, and this direction was before signing the orders (on being mentioned to the court) approved by them.

### Thornton's exors. v. Jett[46]

The award of costs in this suit at the last court being against the testator's estate if sufficient etc., the clerk refused

---

44   Also reported in 1 Va. (1 Wash.) 173 (1793).

45   Also reported *sub nom.* Reynolds v. Waller, 1 Va. (1 Wash.) 164 (1793).

46   Earlier proceedings are reported *supra sub nom.* Thompson v. Jett and in 1 Va.

to tax a lawyer's fee. And application being now made to the court to direct the fee to be taxed, it was refused by the court, whose opinions were as follow. Mr. Mercer was for taxing it. Mr. Lyons would have been for taxing it also but thought [that] the entry, which implied that the suit was on a contract with the testator, made the taxing [of] it improper. Mr. Pendleton was against the motion because he thought that the executors, suing on an assumpsit made to them as executors, ought not to pay costs [any] more than executors suing on an assumpsit made to the testator. But on this point, both Mr. Mercer and Mr. Lyons differed from him.

### Williams and Roy, exors. of Corrie v. Roane, executor of Campbell[47]

[Objection to process; bail]

A writ issued out of the General Court by the appellants against Campbell in case without any endorsement of the cause of action made thereon, which the sheriff executed and took appearance bail. A common order was entered against the defendant, and [the] sheriff, for want of a copy of the bail bond and the order, confirmed. And a writ of enquiry [was] awarded. And in this situation, the said suit, which the declaration showed was in [ ][48], was sent to the district court, where the defendant appeared by attorney at [the] April court [in] 1790 and then consented that the suit should not abate. And a commission was awarded [to] the defendant. Afterwards, at April 1791, the writ of enquiry not set aside on the defendant's motion, the suit was dismissed with costs "for want of endorsement of the cause of action on the writ." And the appeal being reversed in the name of Campbell executor, the court was of opinion that the court below could on a motion made bih [?] proper time inspect the writ and dismiss the suit without [a] plea in abatement or jury, but that as

---

(1 Wash.) 138 (1792).

47  Also reported in 1 Va. (1 Wash.) 153 (1793).

48  Left blank in the manuscript.

to the defendant himself, the motion was too late; he might have made it during the General Court term next after the judgment confessed in the office but not after and that, if he was not precluded by that omission, he would have been so by his appearance afterwards in the district court and not making his objection then. As to the sheriff, he was not obliged to take bail, and there was no pretense to enter judgment against him, either for want of bail bond or for insufficiency of bail; of this judgment, it does not appear that he had notice, but [he] might conclude the contrary by hearing that the defendant had appeared and that the suit was going on between the parties. This being disclosed before executing the writ of enquiry, the court ought to have set aside the judgment as to the sheriff. They might also have set it aside as to the defendant if moved for without bail on his pleading to issue. [It was] reversed with costs with direction to the court to set aside [the] judgment as to the sheriff and proceed to execute the writ of enquiry as to the defendant unless they shall move to set aside the office judgment as to the testator, which they are to do without special bail, plead to issue, and proceed to trial immediately without delay to the plaintiffs on that account.

The court said that, by the law of 1753[49], the sheriff, in cases where bail was not requirable by law on serving a writ, was to take the endorsement of an attorney but by this the sheriff was in a difficulty [?] and might do an injury to [the] plaintiff or [the] defendant by a mistake in his judgment. Therefore, in the Act of 1787[50], the actions in which bail shall be required shall be described, in which trover or any action on the case is not included, unless a judge shall certify it to be so, also those in which bail shall not be required. And as a direction to the sheriff whether bail is to be demanded, every plaintiff, on

---

49   Hening's Statutes, vol. 6, pp. 330-331.

50   Either the Act of 1777, Hening's Statutes, vol. 9, p. 404, or the Act of 1788, Hening's Statutes, vol. 12, p. 740.

pain of having his suit dismissed, shall endorse on the writ the true species of [the] action.

Mr. Pendleton informed me that, in actions of debt, if the causes of action were not endorsed on the writs, proceedings were not to be had against the sheriffs.

## Wilson v. Keeling[51]

[Minutes]

October 1793. [This] was the only cause heard on the 17th. After the cause was opened, Mr. Mercer declined to sit in it and directed himself to be entered absent. At the reading of the orders [the] next day, it did not appear that he had been present at all in court that day, and on that circumstance being mentioned, it was proposed that his name should be entered previous to the adjourning order. He said he was satisfied for the present with the orders and entries but thought that the record ought to show things as they really were and that he ought first to have been entered present and then immediately absent previous to the affirmance in the cause, and to this the court acquiesced.

See [the] proceedings of the 18th for entries agreeably to the above note. Query if he should not also, had he been entered absent before affirmance, have been entered present after it and before adjournment? Yes. See [the] proceedings of [the] 18th.

## Hawkins's exor. v. Beverley[52]

[Executor to pay interest and costs]

In this cause, an objection being made to that part of the judgment of the district court which directs the damages on affirmance and the costs to be levied in case of a deficiency of assets of the appellant's own goods, the court enquired into the practice of the General Court before the war and since

---

51   This case is reported in 1 Va. (1 Wash.) 194 (1793).

52   Also reported *sub nom.* Hawkin's ex'rs. v. Berkley, 1 Va. (1 Wash.) 204 (1793).

and of this court in similar cases and, finding them all to agree with the judgment now appealed from, affirmed the said judgment with damages to be levied according to the directions of the [     ].[53]

[general rule]

On every dismissal of an appeal whether with or without costs, the court directed that an order be made to certify such dismission to the court from whence the appeal came. See [the] proceedings of 19th October 1793 for cases applying to the direction of which the court on reading the orders approved.

### Keel etc. v. Herbert's extrx.[54]

[Executor not to pay costs]

The judgment of the Borough Court of Norfolk and of [the] Suffolk District Court were reversed, and a new trial [was] awarded. The costs in this case were directed to be levied of the goods of the testator only, who was plaintiff in the original suit and who died after the supersedeas issued to the judgment of the District Court, and not in case of a deficiency of the assets of the executor's goods, who was forced into this court by [a] scire facias [and] came in not voluntarily but through necessity.

October 31st 1793. The court directed the reasons to be entered why there was no court on the three preceding days on which a sufficient number of judges did not attend and no adjournment was entered on record; see [the] entry.

### Ronald v. Harmanson etc.[55]

[Supersedeas; scire facias]

At October term 1792, the first writ of supersedeas, which appeared to have been served after the return day was past,

---

53  Left blank in the manuscript.

54  Earlier proceedings are reported *supra* and in 1 Va. (1 Wash.) 138, 203 (1792, 1793).

55  Later proceedings are reported *infra* and *sub nom.* Bently ex'r of Ronald v.

was quashed, and another writ of supersedeas [was] awarded after consideration. At this term the administrator of the plaintiff, who lately died, moved the court for a writ of scire facias to hear errors, which was directed to issue.

### Field etc. v. Spotswood[56]

[Appeals]

The judgment appealed from was entered in the district court the 6th day of October 1792, and the record was returned the 18th June 1793. The clerk, supposing that two terms had elapsed, refused to docket the suit. But the court, on motion, in my absence, directed it to be docketed and considered this [the] second term as the Court of Appeals met in October 1792 before the Fredericksburg District Court adjourned. (By information of Mr. Rob.)

### Jordan v. Neilson[57]

The court awarded a new writ of supersedeas after being informed by Mr. Marshall that one term (to wit April last to which the first writ was returnable) has passed by without any process being awarded, but no argument was had or [any] opinion given on the propriety of the awarding it.

### Byrd v. Cocke[58]

The president was applied to respecting the manner of entering the judgment as to the costs as well as the final part respecting [the] district court's judgment and, on being informed of the direction in *Keel v. Herbert*[59], approved of the entry in this case.

---

Harmanson's ex'rs., 1 Va. (1 Wash.) 273 (1794).

[56] Later proceedings are reported in 1 Va. (1 Wash.) 280 (1794).

[57] Later proceedings are reported in 2 Va. (2 Wash.) 164 (1795).

[58] Earlier proceedings are reported in 1 Va. (1 Wash.) 232 (1793).

[59] *Supra* and 1 Va. (1 Wash.) 138, 203 (1792, 1793).

April Court 1794

### Ronald's admr. v. Harmanson[60]

[Scire facias against administrator]

April 11th 1794. The first writ of supersedeas issued by Ronald was formerly adjudged improperly served and a new one [was] awarded, which was not returned at all. Afterwards, Ronald, the plaintiff, died. A writ of scire facias was awarded [to] his administrator at the last term and returned to this term executed, but the defendants did not now nor had they ever before appeared. The court adhered to the rule established in the case of *Keel etc. v. Herbert's exx.*[61] at [the] April Court 1793 considering the present as a new cause which was not to be tried at this term but by consent. There was this difference between the two cases: in Keel's the scire facias was against the executor at the plaintiff's motion, in the other in favor of the plaintiff's administrator on his motion. Query if the defendants Harmansons had ever appeared before the issuing of the scire facias, whether such appearance would not have so altered the rule as that the cause might have been tried at the court to which the scire facias was returnable without consent? *No, see October 1808.*

### Foushee v. Lea[62]

[Scire facias against an unknown executor]

April 11th 1794. The appellee being dead and his executor not known, the court, on the appellant's motion, awarded a scire facias against the executors. Mr. Lyons observed that, upon the clerk's being furnished with their names, he might insert them in the writ.

---

60 Earlier proceedings are reported *supra;* later proceedings are *sub nom.* Ronald v. Harmanson, 1 Va. (1 Wash.) 273 (1794).

61 *Supra.*

62 Later proceedings are reported in 8 Va. (4 Call) 279 (1795).

## Wallace v. Smith and Moreton[63]

[Relief in equity against surprise]

Case.

A writ was issued in the General Court by Smith and Moreton against B. and B. Piper, one of whom was arrested by Wallace's deputy, but no appearance bail being taken by him, a common order was confirmed against the defendant arrested and Wallace. At the subsequent court, the plea was entered as put in by Wallace, the sheriff, and judgment was afterwards obtained in [the] Fredericksburg District Court against him, and the defendant [was] arrested. To this judgment, Wallace issued a supersedeas from the Court of Appeals. A judgment of affirmance was given, the court seeing nothing erroneous in the record. Wallace then obtained an injunction to stay the execution as to him on the said judgment, and the evidence showed that a bail piece on the suit at law had been offered to the clerk at the rules, which, being thought by him [to be] deficient, was not received, and a common order [was] confirmed against the defendant arrested and the said Wallace, the sheriff, and that, at the subsequent term, the said bail piece was admitted and received by the plaintiff's attorney and a plea [was] directed to be put in for the defendant himself, but that the clerk, not understanding the direction, entered it as through mistake as put in by the sheriff. The injunction was made perpetual in chancery.

And on an appeal from the decree, the court here said that Wallace, instead of proceeding by supersedeas as above, ought to have moved the District Court to have rectified the proceedings as being a surprise upon him not having notice of the plea or other proceedings and that it was the province of the said District Court, upon having the surprise proved to

---

63  Also reported *sub nom.* Smith & Moreton v. Wallace, 1 Va. (1 Wash.) 254 (1794).

them, to have relieved him by setting the matter right, but not having done so, it properly belonged to the chancery court to relieve against the surprise. [The] decree [was] affirmed.

October Court 1794

### William Shermer, heir, exor. and residuary legatee of Richard Shermer, decd. v. Dudley Richardson et al.[64]

[Costs]

Before reading the decree of affirmance in which a blank was left as to the costs, Mr. Marshall for the appellees said that they ought to be given against the appellant, who was plaintiff in the original suit, as he claimed as heir and in his own right as well as executor. But the court directed that costs should not be awarded. Mr. Lyons said that the appellant ought not to pay costs as the claim was for personal estate, which would be subject to the payment of the testator's debts.

### Burnley v. Lambert[65]

[Distribution by executor; waste]

Proof of possession of a slave at the time stated in the declaration though prior to the date of [the] writ [was] sufficient to maintain [an] action unless [the] defendant be legally evicted, which he ought to show. Legacies delivered by executors before debts [are] paid cannot afterwards be claimed by [the] executors or any other. Executors in such case [are] liable on a devastavit to [the] creditor.

### Armistead v. Marks etc.[66]

[Supersedeas by sheriff]

The court adjudged that the sheriff, against whom with another judgment was entered but who was not interested in

---

64  Also reported *sub nom.* Shermer v. Shermer, 1 Va. (1. Wash.) 266 (1794); earlier proceedings are reported in Wythe 159 (1792).

65  Also reported in 1 Va. (1 Wash.) 325 (1794).

the merits, might obtain and prosecute a writ of supersedeas alone and without the other party to the judgment whom he arrested.

## Turner v. Strip[67]

[Validity of a deed improperly recorded]

A deed admitted to record without proper proof was not considered as recorded and adjudged to be void as to creditors and subsequent purchasers but to be a good deed as between the parties and their heirs in this case, no creditors or subsequent purchasers being interested.

## Pleasants & Co. v. Lewis et al.[68]

[Forthcoming bond]

A partial delivery to the sheriff of the property mentioned in a forthcoming bond [was] not a sufficient compliance with the condition, and the bond was adjudged forfeited. The sheriff's proceeding to sell the part of [the] property delivered [was] not deemed improper, and it was ordered that the obligation, on the court below rendering a final judgment on the bond, should have a credit for what the sheriff should have raised by such sale.

## Bruer v. Tarpley[69]

[Mistake of clerk does not invalidate judgment]

The order setting aside the writ of inquiry was concluded with these [words] ("And the order for a writ of inquiry of damages be set aside and thereupon he pleads non assumpsit." The only error alleged was that, for want of a formal conclusion of the plea with the addition of ("And the plaintiff likewise," there was no issue joined. But the court considered

---

[66] Also reported in 1 Va. (1 Wash.) 308 (1794).

[67] Also reported *sub nom.* Turner v. Stip, Lee's reports, *supra*, and 1 Va. (1 Wash.) 319 (1794).

[68] Also reported in 1 Va. (1 Wash.) 273 (1794).

[69] Also reported in 1 Va. (1 Wash.) 363 (1794).

this want of form in making up the issue to be a misprision of the clerk. [The] judgment [was] affirmed.

### Pendleton et al. v. Vandeveer[70]

[Costs taxed to appellant where error in his favor]

The judgment in this case being for a smaller quantity of land than the appellee was entitled to and the error therefore in favor of the appellant, the court directed the appellant to pay costs here. See *Hite v. Matthews*, former court, same case [is] to be considered as a rule established.

### Cosby, Ludoun's Admr. v. Hite[71]

[Amendment of pleadings]

The court determined that, upon any amendment of a declaration, the defendant has a right and ought to be allowed to put in a new plea or to demur without being subject to any creditors previous to being allowed to do so.

### Walden, exor. of Walden v. Payne[72]

[Costs payable out of estate]

Walden, the executor, died pending the appeal, which was revived by consent in the name of John Taylor, his executor. Upon affirmance of the judgment, the court directed the damages to be made of the first testator's estate if sufficient but, if not, then of the second testator's estate.

### Roy v. Garnett[73]

The court directed the costs to be awarded against [the] guardian of the lessors of the appellant as the court below had done.

---

70  Also reported in 1 Va. (1 Wash.) 381 (1794).

71  Also reported in 1 Va. (1 Wash.) 365 (1794).

72  Also reported in 2 Va. (2 Wash.) 1 (1794).

73  Also reported in 2 Va. (2 Wash.) 9 (1794).

## Brock, exor. of Lewis, and Beverley Stubblefield v. Philips[74]

April 16th 1795. Upon my application, Mr. Lyons referred to a former direction of the court, which, he said, directed the decree to be absolute as to the costs. The case he referred to I take to be that of *Wilson etc. v. Keeling* in 1793,[75] the minute of the decree in which shows that such direction was given.

## Hendricks etc. v. Dundass[76]

[Interest; costs]

April 18th 1795. The motion of Dundass to quash an execution against Hendricks etc. was granted by [the] Fairfax [County] Court without costs, which upon an appeal of Hendricks etc. was affirmed by [the] Dumfries District Court with damages and costs. And this last judgment on their further appeal [was] affirmed here.

A question occurred whether so much of the District Court judgment as awarded damages ought not to be reversed, but the court adjudged it to be surplussage as there was nothing for damages to run on.

Another question occurred whether damages on the District Court costs ought to be awarded by this court. Mr. Pendleton thought they ought. Mr. Roane seemed to think [that] damages ought not to be given unless a ("principal sum" as well as costs had been recovered, the words of the law giving damages being ("principal sum and costs recovered." But the appellee consenting to waive any rights he might have to damages and take his costs only, the court left that question to be determined in some future case.

---

74 Also reported in 2 Va. (2 Wash.) 68 (1795).

75 *Supra* and 1 Va. (1 Wash.) 194 (1793).

76 Also reported in 2 Va. (2 Wash.) 50 (1795); earlier proceedings are reported *supra* and 1 Va. (1 Wash.) 92 (1792) *sub nom.* Taylor v. Dundass.

### Fairfax v. The Commonwealth

The court ruled this cause for trial as coming within a clause of the law concerning escheators, which directs a speedy trial, but said that it had been before determined by the court that appeals granted during the sitting of this court should be considered as new appeals to the next term.

### Bernard v. Brewer[77]

*See further*

### [Costs]

October 1795. Upon an appeal from a judgment of the District Court of Northumberland affirming an order and judgment of a county court giving leave to build a mill and awarding costs in favor of the petitioner, on a total reversal in this court, the court said that neither party was entitled to costs in the county court, and therefore those costs were not awarded to the appellant. [This was ruled] on [an] application of the clerk for instruction on that point.

### Collins v. Lowry etc.[78]

### [Costs]

The appellant failed to appear, and the judgment being reserved, the court (on application of the clerk for instruction) directed the judgment to be entered for his costs not to include a lawyer's fee.

### Bernard v. Brewer

*See before*

### [Drafting of orders]

From what fell from the court at the time they gave judgment in the case of *Bernard v. Brewer*, above mentioned, it

---

77  Also reported in 2 Va. (2 Wash.) 76 (1795).

78  Also reported in 2 Va. (2 Wash.) 75 (1795).

seems to be the safer way to insert in orders and judgments made on summary proceedings in which notice is required by law that such notice was given and this whether the person to whom [the] notice was given appeared or not.

## Wood v. Webb

[Scire facias]

The appellant not appearing and the appellee being dead his administratrix appeared and moved the court to revive the appeal and proceed immediately to hear the cause according to the former practice. (See [the] note in [the] case of *Daniel v. Robinson administratrix*[79] in April 1793.) But the court refused to do so saying the case aforesaid, which was read to them, passed without due consideration, and therefore [they] awarded a writ of scire facias. (The case of *Daniel v. Robinson's administratrix* has as much consideration though not by so full a court as this case of *Wood v. Webb*.)

## Gordon v. Frazer etc.[80]

[Writ of error coram vobis; amendment upon motion]

The appellees obtained a judgment by confession *nil dicit*,[81] *see Washington* in [the] Northumberland District Court, which the clerk entered for the principal sum omitting to credit the payments endorsed on the bond *bill penal* and the several warehouses at which the tobacco was payable. To correct these errors, the appellees sued out of the said District Court a writ of error coram vobis, and the court thereupon reversed the said judgment and gave a new judgment for what was then supposed to be the right balance and inserted the three warehouses mentioned in the bill penal, both in the judgment, although the declaration was for tobacco generally, and in the rule for payment of the principal, but omitted a warehouse at which the appellees, by their endorsement on the bill

---

79  *Supra* and 1 Va. (1 Wash.) 154 (1793).

80  Also reported in 2 Va. (2 Wash.) 130 (1795).

81  I.e. default judgment.

witnessed, had agreed to add to the others and also omitted the name of the security for appearance against whom the first judgment was entered.

This second judgment was adjudged by the court here to be erroneous in leaving out the warehouse mentioned in the endorsement which, being witnessed, the court considered as part of the bill penal in giving an over credit to the appellant and awarding costs against him on the writ of error, to which he ought not to be subjected as he was no wise in fault, the mistakes being the clerk's. The president directed the judgment to be entered for tobacco generally as demanded by the declaration but, in the rule concerning the principal, to insert the several warehouses according to the bill penal. The court was of opinion that the error alleged in the first judgment was the misprision of the clerk, which might have been amended on motion, previous notice thereof being given, with more convenience and less costs than by writ of error, which was also proper to correct mistakes of officers as well as errors in fact, that errors of the clerk in business usually left to him which cannot appear officially to the court on reading the orders, the court will correct if discovered to them if the record furnishes anything to amend by, as in this case, the declaration bond and confession of judgment, and that the court can officially correct on reading the orders such things only as have been discussed before them.

## Wroe v. Harris[82]

[Deputy sheriffs]

The order of the county court giving leave to build a mill being reversed by the district court because the inquisition was taken by the under sheriff and not the high sheriff, the appellant appealed to this court, by which the judgment of the district court was reversed and that of the county court affirmed, the court being of opinion that the under sheriff may act and administer oaths for the principal in all cases, those

---

[82]   Also reported in 2 Va. (2 Wash.) 126 (1795).

only excepted which are by law expressly confined to the high sheriff alone.

## B. Payne, exor. of S. Payne v. T. Ellzy[83]

[Executor not to pay costs]

A judgment was obtained in [the] Fairfax [County] Court by the testator against the appellee, from which he appealed to [the] Dumfries District Court. And pending the appeal there, the said S. Payne died, and the appeal was revived in his executor's name. Afterwards, the County Court's judgment being reversed, the executor appealed to this court but, failing to prosecute the appeal, was dismissed with costs. On application to the court, they directed the costs to be levied on the testator's estate only and not in case of deficiency of the executor's estate, who was only endeavoring to complete a suit began by his testator and stood in the same situation as if he had been made a party in this court. See *Keel v. Herbert's exor.*[84] If the executor had begun the suit originally in the County Court, he would not have paid any costs. Query?

## Harrison et uxor, exor. of Minge v. Field, exor. of Field[85]

[Costs]

The costs on the reversal against the appellee who was originally [the] plaintiff, out of the testator's estate only were given by the express direction of the court; by the like direction omitted on dismissing the bill, the reason for deviating from the rule respecting [the] executor was not assigned.

## Harvie v. Borden[86]

A commission to take the examination of a feme covert with the return [was] among the exhibits. An exception was

---

83 Also reported in 2 Va. (2 Wash.) 143 (1795).

84 *Supra.*

85 Also reported in 2 Va. (2 Wash.) 136 (1795); earlier proceedings are reported in Field v. Harrison, Wythe 273 (1794).

86 Also reported in 2 Va. (2 Wash.) 156 (1795).

taken to this commission and return because it did not appear by them that the persons to whom the commission was directed and who executed it were justices of the peace. But the objection was overruled by the court with an observation that, as the law was directory to the clerk and he was bound to direct the commission to justices of the peace, they would presume the persons named therein to be so unless the contrary was proved.

### Drew v. Anderson

[Judgment presumed to be based on evidence]

Cary Drew petitioned for a writ of supersedeas to a judgment of the Prince Edward District Court affirming a judgment obtained against him as deputy sheriff by Thomas Anderson, the high sheriff, in [the] Buckingham County Court on a motion for his proportion of the taxes for 1793 collected in the said county. And among other errors, [he] alleged that the evidence by which the sum was ascertained before the County Court did not appear in the record as in cases of that nature, where the court was to judge without the intervention of a jury, it ought. But the court said that, as in a jury cause, where the evidence does not appear in the record unless introduced by [a] bill of exceptions, every thing is supposed to be proved to establish the judgment, so in this case, the court would have presumed the evidence to have been sufficient as the petitioner, whose business it was to introduce it into the record if he had intended to avail himself of it, had failed to do so, and denied the petition.

April Court 1797.

### Meade v. Jones

[Appeal bonds]

[There was] a petition for an appeal from a decree of the High Court of Chancery dismissing the petitioner's bill of injunction with costs. The petition was granted, and the court directed the bond to be taken in a penalty double the amount of the judgment enjoined, but being informed that the chancellor in granting appeals in similar cases only took the bond to cover the costs, the court directed the bond in this case to be taken in the penalty of £20 only. Upon an inquiry by the clerk, the court also directed that whenever the party praying an appeal did not enter into bond himself and a responsible person gave it, that the responsible person as well as a party was to give security.

## Hudnall's Admx. v. Gordon

[Jury discharged before verdict]

Gordon having instituted a suit against the appellants in the Court of Northumberland County and the suit being at issue, a jury was sworn and sent out of court to consult of their verdict. But before they returned one and before any other entry was made in the cause, the court adjourned till the [next] court in course. At the next court, a jury was sworn and a verdict brought in for the defendants, from which the plaintiff appealed to the District Court. The District Court reversed the judgment of the County Court and sent the same back and, from this judgment, the appellants appealed to this court. Upon the trial in this court, the counsel for Gordon alleged as error in the County Court its having sworn a second jury before the first was withdrawn or discharged. But the court here reversed the judgment of the District Court and affirmed the judgment of the County Court.

## Mills v. Black[87]

[Time for appeal]

May 1st 1798. The appellant being called and not appearing, the appeal was, on the appellee's motion, ordered to be docketed. Afterwards on the 16th May, the court was of "opinion that in this case, in which the transcript of the record was not sent to this court within two terms after the appeal was granted, the court, under the Act of Assembly[88], could proceed no further on the motion of the appellee than

---

[87] Also reported in 5 Va. (1 Call) 241 (1798).

[88] Revised Code of 1792, ch. 63, § 17 (1792) Hening's Statutes, vol. 13, p. 410.

to a dismission of the appeal with costs." And therefore the order of the 1st May was set aside and the appeal dismissed.

[General rule]

October 12th 1798. The President informed the gentlemen of the bar, that the court would hear no cause out of term even by consent except such causes as are brought here for delay, which may be taken up (but in course) when the court is at leisure from other business, but that this rule is not to operate against the trial of a cause out of course for special reasons.

## Craig v. Craig[89]

April 11th 1799. [It was] adjudged that a bond with a condition for performance of covenants was not assignable before the law lately passed authorizing it.

## [Hausmitt v. Bullitt's exors.][90]

[Supersedeas]

Hausmitt's petition for a supersedeas to a judgment recovered in [the] Dumfries District Court against him by Bullitt's executors [was] denied the errors being in form and in favor of [the] petitioners. One of the errors was that the plaintiffs declared for a debt without interest when the declaration showed in a subsequent part that the specialty carried interest. The judgment was for the debt declared for with damages, which appears to have been given in lieu of interest.

## Field v. Culbreath[91]

The clerk added to the judgment in the record that the "defendant prayed an appeal to the Court of Appeals" not stating that the appeal was allowed or that [a] bond was given to prosecute. On a doubt of the clerk as to the propriety of dock-

---

89  Also reported in 5 Va. (1 Call) 483 (1799).

90  Also reported *sub nom.* Hammitt v. Bullett, 5 Va. (1 Call) 567 (1799).

91  Later proceedings reported in 6 Va. (2 Call) 547 (1801).

eting it, the court, consisting of all but Mr. Pendleton, directed it to be done.

### Jones et al. v. Williams[92]

[Appeals]

Mr. Wickham for [the] appellee wished to object to the decree but doubted whether he could do so as he had not appealed. Before he began his argument, he mentioned his wish and doubt to the court, and Mr. Pendleton answered that the court has always in such cases considered the whole case before them on the record and would correct what was wrong as to either party, to which the other judges objected not.

### Fox v. Grigory etc.[93]

[Pleadings; infants]

A suit was brought by the appellees in [the] Williamsburg District Court against John Fox, heir of John Fox, Anne Fox, Henry Fox, and two other children, devisees of John Fox. Against all but Henry, who was not arrested, a judgment was entered at the rules, which was set aside by a plea of payment by the ancestor & *testator* [?] put in by attorney as well for Henry as for the others. Afterwards, on the plaintiff's motion, a guardian was appointed to the defendant Henry, who then for the first time was known to be an infant, and the plea as to him [was] withdrawn. And leave was also given [to] the other defendants to plead a further plea denying assets. And for further proceedings against all the defendants, the suit was sent to [the] rules. A rule was given to plead, but, after no further plea being filed, a judgment by nil dicit was entered against the whole.

To this judgment, John, the heir, being dead, the other parties obtained a supersedeas, on which the Court of Appeals reversed the judgment and remanded the cause for further

---

92 Also reported in 6 Va. (2 Call) 102 (1799).

93 Also reported in 6 Va. (2 Call) 1 (1799) *sub nom.* Fox v. Cosby.

proceedings to be had being of opinion "that there was error as to the defendants John, Anne, William, and T. B. Fox in this, that their plea of payment not having been waived although they had leave to plead at the rules further matter prescribed by the court, the permission was optional in them, and they could not be in default for not availing themselves of it, but on failing to file a further plea, the cause should have been tried in court upon the former issue joined, and that there is also error in the said judgment as to the other defendant, Henry Fox, who, being an infant, is not stated in the record to have appeared by his guardian to defend the suit nor does it appear that the guardian appointed by the court on the motion of the appellees ever acted under or even had notice of such appointment, and therefore, instead of the judgment by default entered at the rules against the infant, a motion should have been made to the court for proceedings against that guardian or the appointment of another for defence."

Mr. Pendleton said that the judgment must be reversed as to John, although no party to the supersedeas, the whole record being before the court and the judgment being erroneous as to him as well as the other defendants. The directions for further proceedings were made general [so] that the court below might do what was right with respect to all the defendants.

## [Noel v. Upshaw][94]

October 16th. In answer to Mr. Warden's further observation to induce the court to revise an opinion of yesterday denying Noel's petition for a supersedeas against Upshaw, Mr. Pendleton said that the court do consider the stay of execution for eleven months by consent as a release of errors.

See [the] form of entry.

---

[94] See also *infra*.

## Williams et al. v. Barbour

[Mistake of date on a bond]

[There was an] appeal from a judgment on [a] forthcoming bond dated 13th March 1798 taken by virtue of an execution dated the "29th December 1798 in the 22nd year of the Commonwealth"; the bond recited the execution as dated the 29th December 1797. Exceptions were filed. The Court of Appeals affirmed the judgment being of opinion that the execution was dated in 1797 and the mistake in the year was set right by the addition of the year of the Commonwealth all the proceedings appearing to have been subsequent to December 29th 1797 and in the 22nd year of the Commonwealth. See [the] copy [of the] record filed with [the] opinions.

## Porter v. Anderson

[Dockets]

[The case was] ordered to be docketed in its proper place, to ascertain which I searched for an appeal from the same district court to the same term of this court and placed it after the latter. Mr. Pendleton said it was rightly done.

## Selden v. King[95]

After a special verdict in ejectment, the defendant died, and a scire facias issued by order of the district court to revive against proper parties, against whom subsequent proceedings were had. And the suit terminated in their favor. On appeal, no objections were made to [the] proceedings, and therefore [they were] supposed to be right; but [the] cause [was] heard on [the] merits. [The] judgment for [the] defendants [was] affirmed. Copy scire facias.

---

95  Also reported in 6 Va. (2 Call) 72 (1799).

## Noel v. Upshaw[96]

[Amended declaration does not require a new plea]

The record in the case of Noel's petition against Upshaw for a supersedeas states a declaration and [a] plea with issue and that afterwards by consent another declaration was filed to stand as the original declaration, but [there was] no new plea. It was objected that no issue was made up because a new plea was not filed. But the President answered that the consent of the parties that the new declaration should stand as the original made the plea to first declaration stand to [the] second, and therefore there was an issue and a new plea [was] not necessary.

(On Noel's petition for [a] supersedeas and in answer to Mr. Warden's observations when the court denied the petition, examine and correct statement.)

## Cook v. Simms[97]

[A] declaration in case in [the] county court [was] entered in four counts, pleas to three first replevied [?] to the second plea [    ] first count to which the defendant demurred on which judgment was given for [the] plaintiff and a writ of inquiry [was ex]ecuted, damages [were] assessed, and judgment [was] given there[on] no notice being taken of the other three counts [    ] the last of which the pleadings did not even [    ].[98]

---

96  See also *supra*.

97  Also reported in 6 Va. (2 Call) 39, 374 (1799, 1800).

98  The rest of the manuscript has been lost.

# DAVID WATSON

David Watson was born at Iona, Louisa County, Virginia, on December 25, 1775. He was the son of James Watson and Elizabeth Shelton Watson. He received a B.A. from the College of William and Mary in 1797 and then returned home to practice law. On February 19, 1801, he married Sarah Minor, the daughter of Garrett Minor; they had several children. He contributed an essay to William Wirt's *The Old Bachelor*. David Watson was elected several times to represent Louisa County in the General Assembly, the first time being in 1801. He also served as a captain in the Virginia militia during the War of 1812 and held the rank of major at his death. He was one of the first members of the Board of Visitors of the University of Virginia. Watson was elected to the state Constitutional Convention in 1829, but he resigned because of bad health without ever attending. He died on January 31, 1830, at his home in Brackettsville in Louisa County.[1]

## WATSON'S REPORTS

Watson's Reports are to be found in a small paper booklet in the David Watson Collection in the Library of Congress, MMC 2514, box 2.

The cases reported were heard in the county courts of Louisa, Goochland, and Fluvanna and in the District Court of Charlottesville. They date from November 1799 to August 1809. Watson does not mention which cases he participated in, but he does mention the following other lawyers: Johnson, Payne, Carr, John Michie, Nelson, P. P. Barbour, J. Barbour, Yancey, Walker, Morris, and Winston.

---

1    M. H. Harris, *History of Louisa County, Virginia* (1936), pp. 70-71, 228, 392, 426, 426A. *Louisa County Historical Mag.*, vol. 9, pp. 72-73 (Winter 1977-1978). J.B. Minor, *The Minor Family of Virginia* (1923), p. 13. C.M. Leonard, comp. *General Assembly of Virginia* (1978), pp. 224, 244, 248, 252, 278, 304, 309, 353. *Calendar of Virginia State Papers*, vol. 10, pp. 437, 481 (1892). F. Norfleet, *Saint-Memin in Virginia* (1942), pp. 85, 220. J. P. Kennedy, *Memoirs of the Life of William Wirt* (1860), vol. 1, p. 266. Watson Family Papers, U. Va. Library MSS. Dept.

November 1799 - November [    ]. Law Notes.

1799. Louisa. November Court Quarter Sessions.

### [Ford v. Gardner]

On [a] motion for [a] new trial in the case of Ford and Gardner respecting a will, it was urged for the motion that, when the jury tried the will, the bill and answer was not allowed to go to them as evidence, which (it was said) ought to have been allowed agreeably to a rule of the High Court of [Chancery] "that in an issue out of chancery, the papers not at the trial shall go to the jury as evidence" or some such words as those. The counsel for the motion urged that they were not acquainted with this rule [    ]. The cause was tried before the jury but had [ ] seen the [    ] made an extract from it and further that in a conversation with Gen. Marshall[2], the General told him that the District Court of Richmond having refused to let the bill and answer go to the jury as evidence, their decision was reversed by the High Court of Chancery. [The] Louisa Court refused a new trial. See [the] report of this case from [the] Court of Appeals by Hening and Munford.[3]

Goochland. November Court Quarter Sessions.

### [Anon.]

A motion was made for taking up an issue out of chancery before other causes which stood before it on the docket. The court determined that it should not be taken up until it came in turn.

### [Anon.]

Where there was a writ of enquiry, the plaintiff dismissed his suit before the writ was set aside and a plea put in. The query was whether a lawyer's fee should be allowed [to] the defendant in his bill of costs. It was urged that the defendant

---

2    John Marshall was a general in the Virginia militia.

3    11 Va. (1 Hen. & M.) 72 (1806).

was not in court until a plea [was] put in, and if he employed a lawyer out of court, the plaintiff would not be charged. It was so considered by the court.

Query: Can [a] defendant recover *any* costs before he enters his appearance?

### [Anon.]

On [a] motion for a continuance on account of the absence of a material witness, it was made a question whether and how often the oath of the party that a material witness is absent (after due diligence to procure him) should be sufficient to put off the trial.

It was urged on one side that a party might always summon such a number of witnesses as to be certain to have some of them absent and then by swearing that [     ] was absent have as many continuances as he pleased.

It was answered that the court had made a rule that not more than two continuances should be allowed for the same cause.

Query: What is the same cause?

1800. Fluvanna. March Term.

### [Johnson v. Jones]

Errors had been filed for this. In an action for malicious prosecution, it appeared that the plaintiff Johnson had been arrested on the information of Jones carried before a single magistrate and dismissed. The jury gave Johnson one penny damages. The declaration stated that the defendant, with intent to injure the plaintiff's reputation etc. "did *endeavor to prosecute* him." It was contended for error that no cause of action was stated in the declaration and further [that] the proceedings actually had in what is called in the declaration a "*malicious prosecution*" did not amount to a *prosecution*, that to make a prosecution, an indictment or information must be found by a grand jury.

The errors were dismissed and [an] appeal [was] taken.

Louisa. May Term.

### Balinger v. Pleasants

The common bail having entered himself special bail without the knowledge of the plaintiff or his attorney, a motion was made by the plaintiff's attorney to set aside the bail as insufficient. The defendant objected that the bail should have been excepted to when offered, that the defendant was not present to procure of her bail, and the bail himself had departed and was not present to establish his own sufficiency. The plaintiff replied [that] it was the business of the defendant to get good bail and that special bail might be objected to any time during the term.

The bail was set aside.

### [ ] Assignee v. [ ] Kimbrough

When the cause was ready for hearing the counsel for [the] defendant moved to amend his plea saying the court had a right to allow it provided he put in an issuable plea. He said something about furthering justice. The other party said the plea must be mentioned that the court might judge whether it was issuable and tended to further justice. The defendant would not mention his plea before the court should grant leave to amend.

The court determined that they would not allow a plea to be added without knowing what it was.

### Anderson v. Kenedy's exrs.

In assumpsit.

It was proved that the executor acknowledged that he believed his testator had received the money without accounting for it. On [a] demurrer, it was argued whether this acknowledgment of the executor was sufficient to prove an assignment by the testator. The court determined that it was.

In the same case, there was this point. The plaintiff had given his bond to the testator; he afterwards paid £40 for which he was to have credit on the bond. The credit was not given. After the testator's death, which was the year after the payment of the £40, the whole was recovered of the plaintiff, he not being able at that time to prove the payment of the £40. It was established by the acknowledgment of the executor as mentioned above. The Act of Limitations was pleaded. It was answered that the action to recover the £40 did not accrue till the plaintiff was compelled to pay the whole bond without credit for the £40, which would bring the cause of action within the time. In favor of the Act, it was urged that the plaintiff ought to have seen that he had credit, and if he had not, his cause of action accrued immediately. The court determined against the Act.

District Court of Charlottesville. Tucker, Judge.

### [Anon. v. Anon.]

An execution issued from the District Court returnable at a day certain. It was levied, and a delivery bond [was] taken, but before the day of sale could arrive, the return day of the execution came. The sheriff returned on the execution "levied on (*certain property*) but not sold for want of time" but said nothing in his return about a delivery bond. The sheriff then took out a venditioni exponas. At the day of sale, the property was not produced, and the sheriff returned on the venditioni exponas "delivery bond forfeited" but did not say when the delivery bond was taken. The court said something about [the] sheriff's amending his return.

### [Anon. v. Anon.]

In an action of trespass for beating the plaintiff's slave, the declaration stated a per quod etc. The defendant contended that the plaintiff in his evidence should be confined to the proof of special damages and compared it to an action in England for beating a servant. But the judge said [it is] not so, for slaves in this country are property. It is therefore like an action in England for injuring personal property so for setting days [?] at the plaintiff's keep etc., and here the plaintiff is not confined to special damages.

And in the above case, the judge remarked that the clause in the Act of Assembly which authorizes ten lashes to be given to a slave found on the plantation of any person not his owner etc. without a note from his master is not applicable when general leave by the owner is to be presumed as where a Negro has a wife etc.

### [Anon. v. Anon.]

In an action against an executor on the plea of fully administered, the point was whether an executor's account settled by commissioners was sufficient evidence to support that plea or whether he should be bound to produce vouchers to substantiate the account in court. The court were of [the] opinion that each item must be proved in court.

1800. Fluvanna.

### [Anon. v. Anon.]

In an action by the master or a person who has harbored an apprentice, it was contended by [the] defendant that the boy was not bound because the indentures taken by the overseers of the poor did not stipulate for freedom dues. It was so determined by the court, but upon exceptions carried up to the District Court of Charlottesville, Judge Jones reversed the decision.

### [Anon. v. Anon., a lunatic]

In the case of a lunatic, Judge Tucker said [that] the suits brought against him were abatable on his becoming insane, so [also] where a man has been seven years absent from the country.

1802. Louisa March Court.

### Wills, assignee v. [ ] Johnson

The case was Freeman, the assignor, sold a mare to [the] defendant, and in [an] action of debt on the bond, [the] defendant's counsel offered for [a] plea (upon setting aside [the] office judgment) "that the bond was given for the purchase of a mare which was sold as a young and good beast whereas she is in fact old and of little value etc." The plea being objected to, the court determined that [the] defendant must put in another before he should be allowed to set aside [the] office judgment.

March Term. Fluvanna.

### [Floyd v. Woodson]

In Floyd v. Woodson, an action on the case, the plaintiff produced a covenant under seal. The court determined that it should not go to the jury as evidence and that no other evidence should be heard because the plaintiff by his own showing ought to have brought a different action and ought to have declared on the covenant.

May Term. Fluvanna.

### Snotgrass v. Tudstall adm'r. of [   ]

After issue, the defendant required a rule to give security for costs. The plaintiff's attorney said enter the rule but it is of no avail after issue joined. The defendant's attorney said the rule would be good and the District Court had allowed it but said there should be no continuance on that account.

### Woodson and wife v. Strange's Exor.

The plaintiff offered in evidence the affidavit of one Willborn who declared that he was indebted to Woodson's wife and that on Woodson's account and, by his directions, he paid the debt to Strange. Woodson, on the trial, wanted credit against Strange for this sum on the evidence of the affidavit. Strange's counsel objected to the affidavit alleging that Willborn was interested. The court excluded the affidavit.

In [the] same cause, it was mentioned that where a single bill stated with "lawful interest till paid," there was no necessity for a writ of inquiry.

### Fitzpatrick v. Frazer

In ejectment.

When the cause was called for trial, the defendant's counsel moved that the court should make an order of survey contending that it was the practice for [the] reason that each party having a copy, the land might be identified and interfering lines might be seen etc. The plaintiff's counsel objected and said the survey was ordered only when necessary, which could not be in this case where the claim was for a certain tract and all or none was to be recovered, and moreover, the present application is too late and evidently with a view to procrastinate.

The court overruled the motion for a survey, and a trial was entered into, a jury sworn, etc.

The plaintiff's counsel read a deed from Benjamin Woodson to Benjamin Fitzpatrick properly recorded etc. The defendant asked for Woodson's title, but the plaintiff went on and offered to introduce oral evidence to prove that the plaintiff had been in possession under that deed and ejected etc.

Here the defendant's counsel contended that a deed is not sufficient evidence of title in [an action of] ejectment unless there has been twenty years possession but that a patent is necessary. For that defendant, possession is sufficient unless the plaintiff makes out a good right against all the world (Espinasse, *Nisi Prius*, page 495) and moved the court to instruct the jury that a patent is necessary.

Johnson, for [the] plaintiff [said that] a deed is considered by the law as a good and sufficient title.

Payne, on the same side [said that] a deed is sufficient without a patent for if a patent were necessary, the plaintiff would be obliged to trace his own title from A to Z before he could recover.

Carr, on the same side, said the motion to instruct is taking the court and bar by surprise. The defendant ought to demur to [the] evidence. Let it be argued before the court.

Oral evidence being here introduced, it accidentally came out that the present defendant had had twenty years adverse possession.

The plaintiff suffered a nonsuit.

## Commonwealth v. Cocke

For shooting at Lynch.

The evidence [was that] Lynch was [the] overseer for Cannon, to whom Cocke had leased his plantation. Cocke came to where Lynch was, in the plantation, and began to abuse him. Lynch endeavored to get out of his way, and Cocke shot at him at the distance of about sixty yards. Lynch was not struck, but the shot hit around him. He could not tell why Cocke shot at him.

The attorney for [the] defendant asked Lynch upon what particular day the assault was made. Lynch said he could not now swear to the particular day, but he knew that the day which he named to the Commonwealth's Attorney at the time he gave [the] information was the right day. But as he could not read or write, he could not say whether the Attorney set the day down right or not.

The counsel for the defendant said to the jury [that] the day was not proven, and as there was no injury, there ought to be no damages.

The jury found a verdict for the Commonwealth of $100.

Counsel for [the] defendant filed errors in arrest of judgment because it was not stated in the indictment that the assault was made maliciously nor within the jurisdiction of the court etc. [It is] to be argued next term.

1802. Louisa. August Court.

## Garritt v. Garritt exr.

In chancery.

It was agreed at the bar that when commissioners had been appointed by a court of chancery and make [a] report, the proper (and perhaps only) way to set aside the report is for the complaining party to file exceptions to the report stating the errors, whether in the conduct of the commissioners or from accident, mistake, etc. It was also stated that after the report had been received by the court, it is too late to file exceptions.

But query if either party had no notice of the meeting of the commissioners or of the return of the report, how could he object until by some legal means he gets notice?

### Banks v. Thomson

It was agreed by the bar that where pending the suit the matter is settled by the parties out of court except as to costs, the court may give judgment for costs without a jury, for, it was said, the jury have nothing to do with costs, but [the] court award them in all cases.

1803. March Louisa Court.

### Thomason v. Trice

In trespass.

It was stated in the declaration that [the] defendant with guns, dogs, sticks, etc. had injured the plaintiff's bull or stag. It appeared from [the] evidence that [the] defendant kept an unlawful fence, that the plaintiff's bull got into [the] defendant's field, and he shot out his eyes.

The jury found a verdict in damages for £4 10$^s$ under the Act of Assembly, ed. of 1794, c. 137.[4] The plaintiff's counsel moved for double damages. The defendant's [counsel] objected that as the Act of Assembly was not declared upon, the plaintiff could not avail himself of it.

Curia advisari vult.

Upon argument at a subsequent term, the court refused to double the damages in the above case.

---

4   *A Collection of All Such Acts of the General Assembly* . . . (1794), chap. 137, sect. 3, p. 284. Also in Shepherd, Statutes, vol. 1, p. 189.

1803. June Louisa Court.

### [Mallory v. Hogan and Mitchell]

In chancery.

The case was Hogan had taken a bond from Mallory for the purchase of land sold by him to M. Hogan, [and he] passed the bond to Mitchell without [an] assignment. A suit was brought in [the] name of Hogan for [the] benefit of Mitchell. Mallory enjoined upon the ground that Hogan had no title to the land and could make him none making Hogan and Mitchell both defendants. Upon the final hearing, Mallory prevailed. The question was of whom Mallory should recover his costs.

It was contended on one side that as Mitchell was, in equity, an assignee and was obliged to try his right at law and failed through the fault of Hogan, the court ought to give judgment for the costs at law against Hogan only and against Hogan and Mitchell for [the] costs in chancery.

On the other side, it was said that as Mitchell was an assignee, he could stand in no better situation than Hogan would have been in if he had brought the suit at law, and had been costs in chancery.

It was further suggested to the court that they might give judgment for Mallory for costs against both and give judgment[5] over for Mitchell against Hogan for the whole costs, and the court decreed accordingly.

1803. August Court Quarter Sessions. Louisa.

### Sprouse v. Cooper

Trespass [for] assault and battery.

The plaintiff introduced a man to be sworn as a witness, to whom the defendant's counsel objected that he was a Mulatto

---

5   "decree over" is written above the words "give judgment" in the manuscript, but the latter were not stricken out.

and by Act of Assembly disqualified to give testimony except between Negroes and Mulattoes.

The plaintiff's counsel said the party objecting to a witness must substantiate his objections by proof of parentage and required of the defendant to prove that the witness was a Mulatto, for in all cases, he that holds the affirmative must prove it; a negative cannot be proved.

The defendant's counsel replied that in some cases the negative is more easily proved than the affirmative, and [so] in this case; for as the defendant could not know beforehand who would be introduced as witnesses for [the] plaintiff, he could not be prepared to support by proof such an objection as the present, and indeed the present objection could in no case be supported by any other proof than the view of the court unless the person objected to had been lately imported from Africa as a slave. If a free man is offered as a witness, no matter how black his complexion and how curly his hair, the defendant or party objecting may not be able to prove his descent, and if, according to the present doctrine, every person objected to on the present ground is to be considered as a good witness until the objection is supported by proof of his descent by the testimony of others as thoroughbred Negroes as any ever imported from Africa must be heard as witnesses where white men are concerned if the party objecting cannot prove by the testimony of others that the witness has one fourth or more of Negro blood in him. The court must judge in this case as in the case of a record plead or infancy.

The court determined by inspection that the person offered as a witness was a Mulatto. The same question had been determined the same way in the same court in the case of *The Commonwealth v. Smith*, where some Miss Ailstocks were offered as witnesses.

### James and Elizabeth Martin v. John Thomson

Elizabeth Martin had obtained a separate maintenance by order of court. Lands had been alloted [to] her, upon which trespass had been committed by Tompson. An action was brought against Tompson, and James Martin was joined with his wife as plaintiff.

In behalf of James Martin, it was moved in court that the suit be dismissed as to him, he having been made plaintiff without his consent, alleging that it was not necessary that he should be joined, the wife having a right to sue by her next friend, and it would be hard that James Martin should be subjected to the payment of costs without his consent, as he would be if the plaintiffs failed in the action.

For William[6] Martin, it was alleged that a married woman could not sue without her husband's being joined in the action and it would be hard on her part that [she] should be left remediless for any injuries she might receive if the husband refused to join in the action, that his being joined in the action was nothing but form, and if it were entered of record that the suit was for the benefit of the wife, the husband could not be compelled to pay costs, and further she was ready to give security for costs if required.

Curia advisari vult.

(Judge Tucker, in his note 19, 1 Blackstone 441, and note 6, 3 Blackstone 94, says there is no court in Virginia which has cognizance of matrimonial causes generally, and divorces a mensa et toro are unknown to our laws, wherefore there can be no suits for alimony in our courts. But from the above case and the common practice of the county courts, it would seem that suits for alimony may be brought in our courts, for these applications by wives for a separate maintenance must be in the nature of suits for alimony as I know of [ ] no act of our Assembly authorizing our courts to hear such applications.

As to the points made by counsel in the case of Martin and wife v. Thomson, ante page 16, they are out of my reading. It is a settled rule of law in England that where a wife has a separate maintenance from her husband secured to her by [a] deed, she may be sued alone. 1 Fonblanque, *Treatise of Equity,*

6  Sic in MS.

109. Espinasse, *Nisi Prius*, 126. And she may sue her husband (by her next friend) in respect of her separate property. But 1 Fonblanque, *Treatise of Equity*, 108; but Mr. Fonblanque, in the same place, doubts whether she can sue any other person without her husband being joined in the action.)

## Pryor v. Kimbrough

In detinue.

In this case, the declaration claimed, amongst other Negroes, one which it appeared had been in the possession of the defendant but was in the possession of the plaintiff at the time of the action brought and had remained in his possession ever since.

The counsel for [the] defendant moved the court to instruct the jury that the action did not lie as to this slave because it was absurd for a man to sue in order to obtain possession of a thing already in his possession and [the] verdict (if he recovered) must be "that the defendant does detain etc." which would be false.

Michie, for the plaintiff, contended vehemently that the action did lie, that the defendant having once had possession, the plaintiff was entitled to damages for that detention, that the jury must find "that he still detains" and must assess the damages, and that if the plaintiff issued his execution for the value of the slave already in his possession, the defendant might have his injunction. He cited 1 Wash. 308, Burnley v. Lambert[7]. He contended that, except in this way, the plaintiff had no remedy for the detention before [the] action [was] brought.

The defendant's [counsel] replied [that] he might recover for the detention before [the] action [was] brought by [an] action on the case.

The court instructed the jury that the action could not lie.

---

7   1 Va. (1 Wash.) 308 (1794).

# DAVID WATSON

April 16, 1803. District Court at Charlottesville. Judges
Tucker and Jones.

## Commonwealth v. Lewis McWain

From Amherst.

On an indictment for murdering Dr. Hopkins.

From an inquest taken on the body of Dr. Hopkins, it was
found that he was killed by the discharge of a gun through a
window in his own house about nine o'clock at night. The
pieces of broken glass fell on the head of his wife, who was
sitting near the window. (I believe there was no person in the
room but himself and [his] wife.) The overseer was asleep in
the next room but did not hear the gun. He was waked by
Mrs. Hopkins's coming to his bed and taking hold of him and
crying that Mr. Hopkins was killed by some person who had
shot him through the window. The overseer hastened to him
and found him dead or just expiring. The shot entered at several places in his breast.

Early next morning, it was discovered by the neighbors
who had assembled that there were the tracks of a man's shoe
in the garden, which had been lately worked. The tracks
came to a fence which divided the yard from the garden
within nine or ten feet of the window through which the doctor was shot. This was immediately suspected to be the track
of the person who had committed the murder, and it was
agreed that no person should go into the garden until the jury
should be discharged from the inquest. The evening before
the murder was committed, there had fallen a light shower of
rain about sunset.

As soon as the jury was discharged from the inquest, several persons went into the garden and measured the track.
They found where it had come and returned through the garden. The shoes appeared from the track to have been half-
soled, and one of them made an impression on soft ground as
if it were run down a little at the heel and at one side. One of
the shoes had a twist to one side (as the witnesses termed it).
This track was followed from the garden to a fence at several

hundred yards distance from the house; at this fence it appeared that a horse had been lately tied. From this place, the track, which had been followed from the garden, proceeded through the fields accompanied by the track of the horse as if the man led the horse. After crossing another fence at a place not used as a common crossing place, as the track of the man could not be seen, the witnesses supposed he rode. They measured the track of the horse. It had shoes apparently half worn on the fore feet but none on the hind feet. The track of the hind feet was remarkable being longer than common and more rounding on the outside than the inside and the points of the feet turning in. These tracks were pursued for more than two miles through very rugged mountains, the man sometimes riding and sometimes walking on account of the difficulty of the places over which he pressed. (The track hitherto pursued was the back track. Why the witnesses pursued the back track was not explained.)

On the top of a mountain, in a small path made by the neighbor's cattle, the back track, which the witnesses were following, was joined by the same track going the way which the back track had come from. It appeared that the person who made these tracks had returned from Dr. Hopkins's to the place where the tracks joined each other by a different route from that which he pursued in going from this place to Dr. Hopkins's. From this place, they followed both the coming and returning tracks to a road, which was used as a common bridle way by the neighbors. Here were the tracks of other horses, but the track pursued was easily distinguished. They traced it almost to Capt. Pollard's fence, the road they were in leading through a lane near to Captain Pollard's house. Here the track appeared to leave the road. Previous to this time, but while they were following the track, some of the company, which consisted of five or six, had observed that the track of the horse was perhaps like the tracks which had been observed to be made by a mare belonging to Lewis McWain, towards whose house, as well as towards others, the road they were now in led. While some of the company were endeavoring to find where the track had gone from the road, some others observed McWain riding along the road towards his home. They called to him, he stopped, and they went up to him.

He immediately asked them what they were looking for. They told him they thought they had followed the track of the horse which was ridden by the man who killed Dr. Hopkins to that place. One or two of the witnesses stated that they thought McWain changed color and appeared much agitated during these remarks. One witness said he was attentive to McWain but did not observe this change of color or agitation. McWain was always of a pale complexion and had naturally a hoarse voice. He complained of having a cold and said he was just returning from the smith's shop where he had heard of the murder of Dr. Hopkins. Some of the company observed to him that his mare appeared to be newly shod. He said yes and that was his business at the shop, she having lost all her shoes except one piece of a shoe. McWain was asked by some of the company if [he] had ridden along that way lately before. He said yes, the evening before on his way to the shop but observing by a rainbow that it was near sundown, he turned back when he got somewhere about the place where they then were. It was now mentioned to McWain that in tracing the track, before they got into this road on the top of the mountain, they had crossed the mouth of a gully in a valley not far from where they then were, in the mouth of which gully there being a considerable quantity of sand or fine dirt, the track of the man and horse were very plainly to be seen. They proposed to McWain to go with some of them and look at this track, and as the way was very difficult, one of the company offered to hold his mare till he walked to see this track. He accordingly left her and went to the gully. As soon as he was gone, his mare was led to a place where her track would appear plain in the road. Upon view and on measuring, the track of the hind foot appeared to be precisely like the track of the hind foot which they had been pursuing. The fore feet having new shoes on were different. While McWain was viewing the track in the mouth of the gully, the tracks then and there made by his shoes were noticed. One of his tracks, which happened to be within eighteen inches of the old suspected track, was marked the moment he took his foot out of it by one of the company with his walking stick that he might be able to know it with certainty. McWain returned to his mare and some who stayed behind measured his track and compared it with the old one. They agreed precisely.

It was now proposed to take McWain into custody, but it being doubted whether they could do it legally not having a warrant, it was proposed privately amongst the company to endeavor to decoy him to go back with them to the place where the murder had been committed. Upon its being proposed to him, he said he had intended to go by from the shop, but it being late, he had determined to go home first and feed his mare and then walk over.

The overseer of Dr. Hopkins, who was present, said if he would go with them now, his mare should be well fed. But he insisted that he would go home first and come over on foot. The pursuers were all on foot, and one of them being unwell, he offered McWain a shilling to let him ride his mare back to Dr. Hopkins's. He refused; the offer was raised to eighteen pence then to a dollar, but he still refused. He was then told that he *must* go but without any direct charge of being suspected. He then said if he must go, he must, but still refused to lend his mare to the sick man.

After proceeding about a quarter of a mile, all the company but one being before McWain, he suddenly turned his mare, bid them "good day," and swearing he would go no further that way, went off in full gallop, some of the company pursuing him and crying "here goes the villain who did the murder." Pursuit, however, was in vain, McWain having the advantage of being on horseback. Some went on to McWain's house; the rest returned to Dr. Hopkins's to give the alarm and to get horses and guns for the pursuit.

When those who went on immediately to McWain's arrived there, they found his mare in the yard with the saddle and bridle on, but he was gone. They saw his gun lying on the joists and desired his wife to give it to them, but she refused. One of the witnesses then went in and took it; upon examining the pan and touch hole of the gun, the witness was of opinion that it had been lately fired, there being the yellow sulfurous stain about the pan, which is common for some short time after a gun has been fired if it is not rubbed off. The gun was not loaded when it was taken by the witness. The pursuers who arrived first at McWain's remained there until a large party collected, but it was now too late to continue the pursuit that evening.

Those who arrived first at McWain's examined the tracks about the yard and stable and found a number precisely like those which had been traced from Dr. Hopkins's through the mountains. The fresh manure about the stable was such as had been found upon the trail through the mountains, and the food scattered about the stable was such as it was pronounced by the company when they found the manure in the mountains that the beast that dropped that manure must have eaten. They saw no tracks of a hoof with a piece of a shoe on. The gun and mare were secured to prevent McWain from getting them.

The next day, and for more than a week after, the mountains in the neighborhood were traversed by numerous parties in search of McWain. Some discoveries were at length made which raised a suspicion that he was harbored at a certain man's house in the neighborhood. This house was watched closely by night until the owner proposed that if the watching would be desisted from, he would lay a scheme whereby McWain should be taken. The person who had watched promised to desist but still continued the watch, endeavoring to do it so as that it might not to be known by the family by whom it was supposed McWain was concealed. In a day or two, information was given by the man at whose house it was supposed he was hid that McWain was ready to give himself up to a magistrate. One of those who had watched attended without a magistrate. He found McWain in the corn house of the man who had given information. He asked the witness to lend him money to fee counsel to defend him. A magistrate came, and he was taken into custody. He looked pale and weak, and being asked what was the matter, he said he had eaten nothing the first three days after he fled.

(Perhaps it was at this time, as soon as McWain was taken into custody, that he confessed that his mare, his shoes, and his gun were used by the murderer of Dr. Hopkins but that he was not the person that used them, that he had lent them to a Negro man belonging to Capt. Pollard, son-in-law to Dr. Hopkins. But as this statement is made from memory without any notes taken at the trial, I cannot recollect certainly whether this confession was made at this time or after McWain was committed to the county jail, nor can I answer for the precise accuracy of every part of the testimony which has been or which may hereafter be stated.)

A witness was introduced who said that five or six weeks before the murder of Dr. Hopkins, he met McWain on the road, and after some conversation, McWain said that he had applied to Dr. Hopkins some time before that for medicine for his family, that the doctor gave him the medicine without charging him anything but told him to go home and work for his family for they stood more in need of the common necessaries of life than of medicine. McWain said he was much offended with the doctor for taking this liberty with him and he was determined to put him out of the way. Upon cross examining this witness, it appeared that he and McWain had been on very bad terms some time before and that the witness had attempted to bind McWain to [keep] the peace.

Another witness swore that about five or six days before the death of Dr. Hopkins, he heard McWain say there was some person in the neighborhood whom he was determined to put to death in less than a week. Upon cross examination, it appeared that this witness too had been at violent enmity with McWain and had actually bound McWain to [keep] the peace about two years before, though the witness himself said that he and McWain were on friendly terms then and at the time when this conversation passed. Being asked what other conversation passed at that time, he said something about a bond which he had been requested by one of their neighbors to give to that neighbor for money due to him, but having heard that this neighbor owed McWain and intended to pass the bond to McWain if it was given, he had refused to give his bond. There was no other person present when this conversation passed between the witness and McWain.

Another witness stated that on the morning after Dr. Hopkins was killed, he went to his still house and saw McWain at the gate near the still house. He went to him and McWain asked him if he had heard of the bad affair that had taken place at Dr. Hopkins's the night before. The witness said he had heard nothing and asked McWain what it was. McWain said the doctor was murdered in his own house by being shot through the window. The witness asked McWain how he had heard of it. McWain said he had been to Capt. Pollard's that morning to feed a colt he had in the pasture there and had heard this news from one of Capt. Pollard's Negro men. Capt. Pollard and his lady were not at home having been sent for in the night, after the murder was committed, to go down to Dr. Hopkins's. McWain wanted to get a little whiskey of the witness, but the witness told him all he had belonged to Capt. Pollard and he could not sell any of it. McWain said Capt. Pollard owed him a little money, and he was sure would let him have the whiskey if he were at home. The witness then set off to go to a neighbor's house towards Dr. Hopkins's and McWain said he was going to the blacksmith's shop and rode some part of the way with the witness.

The blacksmith swore that McWain came to his shop about eight or nine o'clock on the morning after Dr. Hopkins was killed to get his mare shod. When he looked at the mare's feet, he could see that shoes, and as he thought without any doubt, whole shoes, had been lately taken off of both fore feet, and from the appearance of the nail holes and hoof, he thought the mare could not have been ridden farther after the shoes were taken off than about the distance from McWain's to the shop. The smith had heard of the murder of Dr. Hopkins before McWain came. It was mentioned while McWain was present, but he does not know who introduced the subject. McWain mentioned the story he heard from Capt. Pollard's Negro man as has been already related by another witness. The smith said he thought McWain appeared uncommonly restless while at the shop. On account of the wind which blew hard, the shop door was kept shut, and he observed that McWain went very frequently in and out.

Another witness swore that McWain came to his house the day after the death of Dr. Hopkins about ten or eleven o'clock. He asked him if he had been at breakfast; he said not but that he did not want to eat. However, something was set out for him to eat, and he ate a very few mouthfuls. McWain mentioned the murder of Dr. Hopkins. The witness had not heard of it before. He thought McWain appeared uneasy and observed that he was not willing to say much about the death of Dr. Hopkins. The witness frequently mentioned it, but McWain would always take the first opportunity of changing the subject. McWain stayed till about three or four o'clock in the evening without mentioning any business at the witness' house, nor did the witness know of any that brought him there.

After McWain was committed to jail, he was visited by a witness who swore that on his stating to McWain the enormity of the crime of murdering so good a man as Dr. Hopkins, McWain said, "If I had been sober, no man could have got me to do it." The witness said he thought that when McWain said this, he was in a way to make confessions, and as he did not wish to hear them, he left him without further conversation.

(While McWain was in the county jail, he told some stories which raised a suspicion that Capt. Pollard was concerned in the murder of Dr. Hopkins. Pollard was taken up and examined by two justices of the peace, and on this examination, McWain was brought out as a witness against him. One of the magistrates was called on the trial of McWain in the District Court to give evidence as to what McWain testified on the examination of Pollard. McWain's counsel made it a question with the court whether anything said by McWain as a witness against Pollard could be given in evidence against McWain. The court asked the magistrate whether McWain gave testimony against Pollard freely and voluntarily and without promises or threats of any kind being made to extract his testimony. The magistrate said [that] he testified freely and voluntarily, without promises or threats. The court directed the magistrate to proceed with his testimony.)

The magistrate then stated the purport of what McWain had testified on the trial of Pollard before two magistrates. It was a long story about Pollard's persuading him, McWain, to kill Dr. Hopkins and that McWain had once agreed to it and afterwards refused. A few days before Dr. Hopkins was killed, Pollard again applied to him, and he agreed to do the deed. They went with a Negro man of Pollard's and McWain's mare and gun. Pollard had a Bible and [a] bottle of spirits. He swore McWain to ask him no questions. When they got near to Dr. Hopkins's, McWain's heart failed him, and he refused. Pollard said it must be done. He took McWain's shoes and gun and went from him. McWain heard a gun. Pollard returned to him [and] gave him his shoes and gun. They met at the place where McWain's mare was tied, etc., etc.

Several different stories containing different and contradicting confessions of McWain were related in court.

Some evidence was given concerning Dr. Hopkins's will. It appeared that there was a report in the neighborhood that by the will, Dr. Hopkins's slaves were to be free at his death, and it was urged by McWain's counsel that this might have been heard of by the slaves and have been the cause of his murder.

On the other hand, it was suspected that Pollard, who married Dr. Hopkins's only child and was not on good terms with the doctor, suspecting the contents of the will to be unfavorable to him and having great influence over McWain, who was a man of bad character, had procured him to murder the doctor, then he, Pollard, might destroy the will, etc.

McWain was found guilty by the jury, sentenced to be hanged, and executed accordingly.

1804, April 21st. District Court, Charlottesville.

Carrington, Judge.

### Tucker v. Edmonds

An order of reference had been made in this cause and afterwards a rule to give security for costs. When the cause was called again, a motion was made to dismiss it, no security having been given, Nelson, against the dismission, said [that] the order of reference had removed the cause to another tribunal and the rule for security was improperly made and ought to be set aside.

The court said [that] the cause was not so removed but that it was still under the control of the court, and it must be dismissed.

### Betsy Davis v. William Moon

Assault and battery.

The defendant moved for a rule to give security for costs according to a late Act of Assembly.[8]

The court required an affidavit in writing.

The counsel for [the] defendant said the practice [was] new and wished to know what the affidavit should contain to support the motion for security.

The court said "File your affidavit, and the court will judge of its sufficiency." The affidavit was filed and sworn to by the defendant stating that the plaintiff was too poor to pay costs, was an itinerant person, of a quarrelsome disposition, and had great malice against the defendant, and had provoked the defendant to strike her by making the first assault herself, etc.

The court said if those circumstances were sworn to by a disinterested person, perhaps the rule would be granted.

[An] affidavit was accordingly made by a person said to be disinterested. It was then discovered that the cause stood on a

---

8   Act of Dec. 1802, chap. 6, Shepherd's Statutes, vol. 2, p. 407.

writ of enquiry. The court said the defendant could not ask for a rule before he was in court. The defendant's counsel set aside the writ of enquiry and pleaded.

The court then said the plaintiff should not be procrastinated by this motion. If the parties were ready for trial, it should be had without making the rule, but if the cause was continued, he would then hear counsel on the subject of security for costs.

It is said [that] the rule that the plaintiff shall not lose a trial by being ruled to security after the cause is set for trial holds also in the case of the plaintiff's not being an inhabitant of this state.

### [Anon. v. Anon.]

When the jury were going out on a writ of enquiry, the court said the proper verdict would be to find the interest in damages and find nothing else, for the plaintiff has a judgment for his debt already.

I suppose this is the case where the debt is due by [a] single bill.

Louisa. April Court.

### James McGehee v. William McGehee

On [a] motion for leave to build a mill, on the return of the inquisition, it appeared on the face of it that three of the jury did not agree with the other nine, these three being of [the] opinion that the health of William McGehee's family would be injured but agreed as to all other facts.

Yancey moved to quash the inquisition.

P. P. Barbour, for James McGehee, contended that the court were not bound in any case by the inquisition but might hear other evidence (read the law) and offered to prove that no injury would arise to William McGehee.

Yancey, contra, said the court might hear other evidence against building a mill after the jury had reported in favor of building, but the court can never grant leave to build until a jury has found an inquisition in favor of it, and in the present case there is no verdict, the jury not having agreed.

The court quashed the inquest.

May, Louisa Court.

### Crew v. Tisdale

On a writ of enquiry [?].

The writ in this suit was returned to [the] November court. At this term, the defendant appeared and offered for [a] plea the Act of Limitations. The plaintiff's counsel objected to that plea saying it was a plea not favored in law, and the District Court had decided that if the defendant neglected to plead at the first term after that to which the writ was returned, he should not put in that plea nor any plea which did not go to the merits. The court did accordingly.

1804. September. District Court of Charlottesville. Parker and Stewart, judges.

### Gilmer's exrs. v. Bruce[9]

An action of debt had been originally brought against two defendants. The writ was executed on one and an alias on the other. [There was an] office judgment against the first, execution, and [a] delivery bond, and judgment on that. The suit going on against the first defendant, when it was called this term, the plaintiff said it must be dismissed and asked for his costs. There was some objection by [the] defendant's counsel on the ground that the plaintiff had two suits at the same term for the same debt, and as by [the] delivery bond, the debt was secured against one, he ought not to have costs against the other. The plaintiff said this was the first term which had arrived since the debt had been secured by the delivery bond and asked for costs up to this time.

The court said the plaintiff had a right to pursue both defendants till the debt was paid or the parties were changed by

9    This case is also reported in Yancey's reports.

the delivery bond, which was a new security for the debt; he ought then to dismiss his suit as to the other defendant, but as this is the first term since the new security, the plaintiff must have his costs up to this term.

### Barnett v. Chewning

In ejectment.

The plaintiff produced in support of his title a deed from Thomas Wash and the will of Thomas Wash's father devising a tract of land (of which that now in dispute is said to be a part) to three of his sons. The will directed the tract to be equally divided between them. It also directed the manner of laying it off and the particular lot which each son should have. One of the sons was called to prove that the land had been divided according to the will and that Thomas had received and had possession of the lot now in dispute. He also proved that there had been an uninterrupted possession by his father, his brother, and the plaintiff for more than twenty years before the defendant got possession.

Several doubts were raised by Walker for the defendant: first whether the plaintiff must not prove twenty years possession in *himself*, and second if he were allowed to avail himself of the possession of those under whom he claims or whether in the present case there had not been an interruption of possession in the passage from Wash, the devisor, to his son Thomas inasmuch as Thomas could not be said to be possessed of the land now in dispute until after the division and its mutual ratification among the brothers, which ratification, he also contended, must be by mutual releases in writing.

The court hooted at the doubt "whether the plaintiff could avail himself of the possession of those under and through whom he claimed," and as for the suggestion in this case of an interruption of possession till the division among the three brothers, there was no interruption for after the death of the father and until the division, each of them might be said to be possessed of the whole. As for the necessity of written releases, if there was no objection made to the division and each took possession of the part devised and laid off to him and exercised acts of ownership over it, it was a sufficient ratification of the division.

[There was a] verdict and judgment for [the] plaintiff.

## [Anon.] and Co. v. Jones[10]

Motion [for judgment] on [a] forthcoming bond.

The counsel for the defendant moved the court to quash the bond and the execution on which it was taken it appearing that the execution issued from the District Court office and was so made returnable on the face of it to the first day of July, which was a day previous to the commencement of the next term, and, by reference to the almanac, the first day of July, the return day of the execution, was [a] Sunday. The Act of Assembly, R.C., c. 249, s. 1,[11] provides that "executions hereafter issued from a district court may at the election of the party suing out the same be returnable on the first day of the next court of such district or to the clerk's office on the first day of any month previous thereto *unless that shall happen on a Sunday*, in that case the same shall be returnable the next day." Under the authority of this law, the execution issued, and by this law, the counsel for the defendant contended that it was void, having been made returnable on the first day of the month which happened on Sunday. Whereas in that case it ought to have been made returnable on the second day of the month, and the execution being void, the bond taken under it, upon which the present motion was made, was also void, and a motion for judgment upon it could not be sustained.

The court said [that] the execution was not void, that the provision of the law directing that where the first day of the month happens on a Sunday, the execution shall be return-

---

10  This case is also reported in Yancey's reports.

11  *A Collection of All Such Acts of the General Assembly* . . . (1803), p. 390. Also in Shepherd's Statutes, vol. 2, p. 151.

able on the next day was made from respect to the *day* and not for the advantage or disadvantage of either party, that though the clerk makes the execution on the face of it returnable to the first day of the month, yet when that day arrives, if it happens to be [a] Sunday, the law itself makes it returnable the *next* day, it does not say that the clerk shall *make it* returnable the *second day* of the month, that the intention of the legislature seemed to be that where the execution is by the clerk *made* returnable to the first day of any month, if when that day arrived, it should happen to be [a] Sunday, the sheriff shall be allowed to return it the next day and his return on that day shall discharge him.

The defendant then offered to prove that he had complied with the condition of the forthcoming bond and that the sheriff's return that the bond had been "forfeited" was false.

The counsel for the plaintiff made it [a] question with [the] court whether, as the sheriff's return was upon oath, the truth of it could be contested in this summary way and whether the party aggrieved by the return ought not to be confined to his action for a false return.

(From the case of Pleasants & Co. v. Lewis, 1 Wash. 274,[12] it seems that the defendant was allowed by the district court to contest the truth of the sheriff's return at the time when [the] motion was made on the forthcoming bond, and no objection [was] made to it by the Court of Appeals. See also Nicholas v. Fletcher, 1 Wash. 330.)[13]

The court [said that] the sheriff's return is prima facie evidence of the breach of the condition, but on a motion for judgment grounded on the breach, the defendant shall be allowed to prove a performance; it would be hard that his property should be sacrificed in this summary way and that he should be sent to the tedious redress of an action at law. But as the interest and character of the sheriff was [ ]ply in-

12   1 Va. (1 Wash.) 273, 274 (1794).
13   1 Va. (1 Wash.) 330 (1794).

vol[ ] in the question, he should not be surprised into a trial of the question, but the motion shall be continued till the next term if he desires it.

The motion was continued till two days after, and I was informed that the question between the defendant and sheriff would be "how long the *day* for the forthcoming of the property lasted," the sheriff admitting that the property was produced after *sunset*, which he contended was too late. The defendant contended that the property was delivered before sunset, but that if the sun was down, it might be well delivered afterwards. How far he meant to contend the day extended for a delivery, whether till dark or twelve o'clock at night, I do not know.

Query: If the decision was right in allowing the defendant to prove performance in that summary way and thereby convicting the sheriff of a false return?

And query: If, in an action against the sheriff for a false return, this decision of the court in this case could be given in evidence against him?

### [Anon.] v. [Anon.]

On [a] motion [for judgment] on a forthcoming bond, the condition [of which] said "that whereas an execution had issued etc. which execution etc. amounting to the sum of one hundred and fifty and twenty five cents" omitting the word "dollars" after "one hundred and fifty," it was contended that this omission was fatal and the motion not sustainable.

### [Anon.] v. [Anon.]

Motion [for judgment] on a forthcoming bond.

The defendant moved for a rule for the plaintiff to give security for costs on the grounds that he was not an inhabitant of this state. It was replied for the plaintiff that the law authorizing a rule for security for costs did not apply to motions on forthcoming bonds and that Judge Tucker (while on the District Court bench) had so determined. This court granted the rule but said the motion should be continued to allow the plaintiff time to give security. [See] ante page 8, Snotgrass v. Tudstall.[14]

Query: Whether the words of the law "every action at common law or suit in equity" R.C., c. 76. s. 23[15]can be construed to include a motion [for judgment] on a forthcoming bond? See The Auditor v. Graham, 1 Call 477[16] Motions [are] included in the terms suits and actions in some cases.

Louisa. November Court 1804.

### Trice v. Edwards (or Edwards v. Trice)

A witness being called to the book, the party against whom he was summoned had him sworn to answer questions and asked in the usual manner if he was not interested. He swore he was not. Other witnesses were then examined to prove that he was interested. Though this was warmly objected to by P. Barbour saying that, as the party against whom the witness was called has chosen to have him sworn on the voir dire, he ought not to introduce other evidence to set him aside though he might call other witnesses to invalidate his testimony, the court, however, being satisfied that the witness was interested, would not allow him to be examined.

1805. March, Louisa Court.

### Travilion v. Morris

Case.

It was in evidence that Barnet had built a mill on the South Anna River by an order of [the] Louisa Court in the year [ ]. An acre of land had been taken by ad quod damnum from G. Bell for an abutment for the dam. The mill house was placed at first on the opposite side from the condemned acre. The f[ ]shes having afterwards injured the situation, Barnet moved

14  See above.

15  *A Collection of all Such Acts of the General Assembly*...(1803), p. 111. Also in Shepherd's Statutes, vol. 1, p. 32.

16  5 Va. (1 Call) 475 (1798).

the dam lower down the river without any new order of court and placed the house on the side of the river next to the acre condemned from Bell. There appeared to be some doubt whether the dam as now situated touched the acre condemned for the abutment or not. But from the best evidence, it seemed that it did. Travilion purchased this mill as it now stands from Tisdale, who purchased of Barnet.

A mill was built before the year 1748 at a place below Tisdale's at a seat called the old Bird. Some years after the mill, now Tisdale's, was built, the Bird mill was suffered to fall. The seat was sold from one to another till it became Garth's, and he got an order for a jury to view etc. in order to rebuild. The petition and order proposed a dam of eleven feet. Morris afterwards purchased the seat and built a mill without having finished the proceedings under the order last mentioned. The backwater of the old Bird Mill never flowed within less than three quarters of a mile of Travilion's present mill. Morris raised his dam thirteen feet three inches five eighths and covered Tisdale's tub wheel. For this the present action was brought.

Upon the trial, it was contended for Morris that the old Bird Mill having been built before the acts of Assembly regulating the building of mills passed, the seat could not be affected by anything contained in those acts, that the seat could never lose its privilege of rebuilding by the mill's being suffered to fall, nor could there be any restriction as to the height of raising the dam, notwithstanding the mischief it might do to the lands and improvements on the stream above.

Morris's counsel moved to instruct the jury that Tisdale's action could not be maintained unless he proved a freehold title to the land on which his [    ] mill stands. The court refused to give such [an] instruction.

They then moved for leave to introduce evidence to prove that the title was not in Tisdale nor in any person under whom he claimed. The court refused, and Morris's counsel excepted etc.

The jury brought in a verdict of £265 damages. [There was an] appeal.

### [In re] John Boswell's Will

After disposing of his soul etc. "and as for such worldly goods as it hath pleased God to bless me with after all my lawful and just debts are paid, I will and dispose of the remainder in the following manner that is to say I give to Boswell Thornton the land etc. and the following Negroes etc. etc." Query as to [the] liability of [the] estate to pay debts.

District Court of Charlottesville. April Term 1805. Judges Tyler and White.

### Hart, surviving pat. etc. v. Rob. Nelson admx. etc.[17]

The case was that a suit had been brought in the County Court against the administratrix and judgment obtained to be satisfied out of the goods etc. when they should come to her hands. Upon this judgment, a scire facias was issued summoning the administratrix to appear and show why execution should not be awarded, but the scire facias did not suggest that goods etc. had come to her hands to be administered etc. since the rendition of the judgment. Execution went by default on the scire facias and was returned nulla bona.

The present action was to convict the administratrix of a devastavit. The declaration stated the proceedings in the court below and, reciting the judgment, said that "by the consideration of the court etc. the plaintiff recovered etc." But the copy of the judgment produced said it is "ordered" by the court that the plaintiff recover etc., the word "ordered" being used instead of "considered." Nelson, for [the] defendant, said no circumlocution could supply the words ideo consideratum est. The court were of the same opinion and withheld the judgment from going to the jury.

Nelson also contended that as the first judgment was to be satisfied when assets should come to the hands of the admin-

---

17   Also reported in Yancey's reports and below.

istratrix, the plaintiff in this action must prove that assets had come etc.

The court asked if the scire facias suggested that assets had come etc. and it appeared that it did not. The court said [that] then it is necessary to prove it.

A juror was withdrawn, and the cause [was] continued [so] that the record might be amended as to ideo consideratum and if it was an error in copying.

District Court of Charlottesville. April Term. 1805.

## Commonwealth v. Jesse Dixon[18]

On [an] indictment for forgery, Dixon was charged in the indictment with forging a note for the payment of money purporting to be given by Chilows to Brady.

It appeared from the note produced in evidence and said to be forged that the note had been assigned by Brady to Dixon and by him to Birch. The assignment by Brady was a forgery, Brady swearing that he never had any such note from Chilows nor did he ever assign any such to Dixon.

Chilows was called to prove that his signature to the note was forged. Birch had given his testimony before. The counsel for [the] prisoner objected that all the witnesses were incompetent being interested. Chilows alone was excluded by the court because he being [the] obligor in the note, it was his interest to prove it [to be a] forgery. One of the court [said] if the prisoner was convicted, the note would be destroyed. The assignor Brady was admitted, the prisoner not being charged with forging the assignments, and Birch, if he established the forgery, would be swearing against himself.

---

18   Also reported in Yancey's reports.

## Hawkins' admr. v. Barclay's devisees[19]

Debt on a bond.

[There was a] plea [of] payment.

The court said [that the] defendant holds [the] affirmative and has the right to open and conclude the argument.

In this case, the defendant relied on [a] presumption arising from the bond having been more than twenty years due before [the] action [was] brought. It was made a question with the court whether the five years, five months, and seventeen days to be taken out [of] the Statute of Limitations in certain cases by Act of Assembly [applies].

The court said [that] in an equitable construction of the Act, this time ought to be taken out, for the same reason applies in both cases.

## Hart surv. p. v. Rob. Nelson admr. etc.[20]

A record from [the] Louisa Court was declared on and the declaration reciting the judgment stated that "it is considered" by the court that the plaintiff recover etc. Upon inspecting the record, it appeared that the record of the judgment stated "therefore it is ordered by the court." Counsel for [the] defendant objected to the record going to the jury because no words could supply the place of "ideo consideratum est." The court were of that opinion and that the record was bad.

The suit in the County Court was brought against the administratrix and the judgment was to be satisfied out of the goods etc. of [the] intestate when they should come into the hands of [the] administratrix. A scire facias was issued against her summoning her to appear and show what had come to her hands to be administered since the rendition of the judgment, but the scire facias did not suggest that other

19  Also reported in Yancey's reports.
20  See above and Yancey's reports.

goods etc. had come to her hands etc. since the rendition etc. Execution was awarded on the scire facias by default and returned nulla bona. The present action was brought to convict her of a devastavit.

Counsel for [the] administratrix contended that [the] plaintiff must prove a devastavit by other evidence than the return on [the] execution on [the] scire facias.

So said the court because, if the scire facias had suggested that goods had come to her hands, she must have pleaded that no goods etc. had come etc. But her silence should not be admitted to prove a fact which was not stated in the scire facias.

### Dickison, admr. of Matlock v. W. Chisholm admr. etc.[21]

Debt on a judgment.

The declaration stated a judgment to have been obtained for a sum (viz. £100). Upon [a] view of the judgment, it stated a recovery for so much, but [it was] to be discharged by a smaller sum. This condition in the judgment not being mentioned in the declaration was considered as [a] variance, and the plaintiff suffered a nonsuit.

### Philips' admr. v. Meriwethers, securities [for] Meriwether, deputy sheriff for Philips

On [a] motion [for judgment].

A notice was read [?] given to the deputy's securities, he not being included in the notice.

Nelson for [the] defendant contended [that] the notice [was] not sufficient to sustain the motion as the deputy ought to have been included for he is the proper person to defend the motion. They relied also on the words of the Act giving the remedy to the high sheriff against his deputy.

---

21 Also reported in Yancey's reports.

## Philips' Will; Marshall's Opinion.

"I give to my son John the land whereon he lives also Negroes E[ ] etc. provided he has a child, but in case my said son John should have no child, what I give him my desire is that the same shall be equally divided [?] between my son[s] George and William. I desire that all my other estate, be it whatsoever, I give to be equally divided among my sons George, John [and] William with the proviso respecting my son John, that is to say, in case my said son John should die without child, the estate given him to be equally divided between my sons George and William."

John having died without a child, the land and Negroes given [to] him will be divided equally between George and William. J[ohn] Marshall.

## John Hopkins' Will[22]

1807. September Term. District Court of Charlottesville. White, Judge.

### [Anon. v. Anon.]

On a motion [for judgment] on [a] delivery bond, P. Barbour, on behalf of the plaintiff, [argued that] the sheriff had returned on the execution "Executed on the property of A and B and delivery bond taken," but [he] had not mentioned on the execution the particular property on which it was levied, but in the forthcoming bond, the property was specified. The court said it was good, the endorsement on the execution by the sheriff having reference to the delivery bond. Query?

---

[22] This extract has not been transcribed since the reporter gives no comments upon it.

### [Anon. v. Hunton]

Motion [for judgment] on [a] delivery bond against Huntons.

The execution was against the property of three, Charles, Thomas, and their mother. The delivery bond in reciting the execution mentioned only Charles and Thomas, and the mother was the security to the delivery bond. The court said [that] the recital was incorrect; and the delivery bond not agreeing with the execution, the motion was overruled.

### [Anon. v. Anon.]

Motion [for judgment] on [a] delivery bond.

The execution had been levied on sundry property amongst which was a cow. A forthcoming bond was taken, and being credited by the price of several articles which were produced at the day of sale and sold, it was returned "forfeited," the cow having died before the day of sale, though her skin was produced and sold.

For the motion, it was argued that by the express words of the law, the goods were to remain in the possession of the debtor *at his risk*; and therefore nothing but a delivery of them according to the bond could discharge the obligation, no matter by what inevitable accident the delivery might be prevented.

(A case was mentioned, though not in court, of a rise in a river which put it absolutely out of the power of the debtor to produce the property, and yet the court gave a judgment on the delivery bond as forfeited.)

Judge White said [that] the act of God should injure no man, and if the condition of a bond became impossible before the day of performance by any unavoidable accident, the obligor would be considered as discharged from the condition. But he would consider of the case and hear anything the bar might wish to say on the next day.

I heard no more of it in court.

Out of doors, it was argued that the forthcoming bond being a discharge of the former judgment, if the plaintiff did not get his debt under the forthcoming bond, he could not take out another execution. But this [is] not true, for the former judgment is not discharged by the giving of a forthcoming bond but its forfeiture, and if the bond is discharged without being forfeited, that is, if the bond is complied with or the obligors released from the condition of complying with it, the plaintiff may proceed on his judgment to take out other executions for what may remain due.

1809, August, Louisa Court.

### Purrington v. Bane

Ejectment.

Bane had given a deed of trust to Minor and Garth to secure the payment of a debt due [to] Mitchell. The conveying part of the deed was to Minor and Garth and their heirs etc. with a power to them or either of them to sell in case of nonpayment by the day after advertising three weeks in some Richmond newspaper, but in case the debt should be punctually paid, the deed was to cease and the said Minor and Garth were to reconvey to Bane.

The debt was not paid, and Garth, one of the trustees, advertised the land to be sold for ready cash, and Dickison was the last bidder, and the land was knocked out to him. Garth, not having a deed ready to convey to Dickison, did not demand the money, supposing Dickison would pay at any time when a deed should be tendered to him. A few days after the sale, Mitchell's agent called on Dickison for the money, but he could not pay it and said they might sell the land again. It was advertised again, and Purrington became the purchaser. And this action was brought to get possession from Bane.

At the trial, it was testified by one witness that he had seen in the office of the *Enquirer* a file of newspapers containing a regular insertion of the advertisement of the last sale according to the terms of the deed, and several detached *Enquirers* were produced in court containing the advertisement, and it was proved that the sale took place on the day and on the terms mentioned in the advertisements.

The defendant's counsel moved the court to instruct the jury that no parol evidence ought to [be] taken to prove the regular publication of the sale but that a regular file of the newspaper ought to be produced to the jury. The court overruled the motion, and the defendant's counsel excepted.

It was also in evidence that Garth alone made the sale and that the conveyance to Purrington was made by him only, Minor's name not being mentioned in the conveying part of the deed nor his name signed to it.

The defendant's counsel moved the court to instruct the jury that, as the deed of trust conveyed the land to Minor and Garth jointly and though it empowered either of them to sell, [it] nowhere gave to either of them the power to convey and more especially as in case Bane paid the debt punctually, the said Minor and Garth were to reconvey the land to him, the deed made to Purrington by Garth alone was not sufficient to give him the legal title to the land. The court refused to give such [an] instruction to the jury, to which opinion the defendant's counsel also excepted

The jury found for the plaintiff.

J. Barbour and Michie [were] for [the] defendant. Poindexter [was] for [the] plaintiff.

### [In re Will of George Bell]

George Bell by his last will and testament, after sundry devises to his other sons, devises as follows, "I give and bequeath to my son Pleasants the land that I lent to my wife containing 150 acres to him and his heirs and further my will is that if either of my said sons should die without lawful issue that the part allotted to them be equally divided among the surviving brothers."

J. Michie: The question proposed is "whether Pleasants takes a fee simple in this land after the devise to the wife or is the devise over to the other brothers good?" I am of opinion [that] Pleasants takes a fee simple subject to the devise to the mother and that the devise over on the contingency of his dying without issue is too remote so that a joint deed from Cecily and Pleasants Bell will convey a full and absolute estate in [the] said land. John Michie.

Louisa Court.

### Pulliam's Exex. v. Pulliam

In debt.

This was an action brought by Sarah Pulliam, executrix of Jennings Pulliam deceased (who was one of the executors of John Anderson deceased) against Anderson etc. John Anderson and Jennings Pulliam qualified as executors of John Anderson. A bond was taken by Jennings Pulliam to himself only as executor of John Anderson deceased. Jennings Pulliam died, and Sarah Pulliam qualified as his executrix and brought this action on [the] said bond, John Anderson, executor of John Anderson deceased, being still alive.

Morris, for [the] defendant, pleaded specially that this action cannot be maintained by an executor of an executor of the deceased while an original executor is still alive.

Winston, for [the] plaintiff, demurred to the plea contending that, as the bond was given to Jennings Pulliam only, it was different in law from what it would have been if given to both executors, and in the present case, John Anderson, the surviving executor, could not sue on the bond, his name not being mentioned in it.

The court overruled the demurrer being of [the] opinion that the action was not sustainable.

1809. August Term. Fluvanna.

### Cheatham v. Tilman

Libel.

On the fifth day of the court, for particular reasons, the court determined to take up this cause out of its turn, there being many causes on the docket before it. The plaintiff's counsel objected and excepted etc. The cause stood on [a] writ of enquiry. The defendant, after the court had determined to try the cause, pleaded "not guilty and justification." The counsel for the plaintiff then insisted on a continuance as a matter of right. The court said "try the cause." The plaintiff excepted etc.

# DAVID YANCEY

David Yancey was born at Yanceyville, Louisa County, Virginia, and lived there his entire life. He received a B.A. from the College of William and Mary in 1796.[1] He was engaged in the practice of law in November 1801[2] and was probably admitted to the bar a year or two earlier. In July 1800, he married Ann Minor, the daughter of James Minor, but she died on March 2, 1805, at the young age of 20;[3] there were no children. He was a lieutenant in the Louisa County militia in 1804.[4] In a letter to a friend, Peachy R. Gilmer, in February, 1807, he indicated that his practice was going well. However, another letter to Gilmer dated August 22, 1807, from Red Sulphur Spring indicated that he was seriously ill; he wrote that if he was not cured there, he would go to a warmer place.[5] In September he requested a passport.

Yancey wrote a codicil to his will on December 7, 1807, and the Richmond newspapers reported his death in Jamaica sometime before January 30, 1808.[6] He probably died of tuberculosis, probably in his early thirties.

---

[1] M. H. Harris, *History of Louisa County, Virginia* (1936), pp. 228, 438, 438A. "Letters from William and Mary, 1795-1799," *Va. Mag. Hist. Biog.*, vol. 30, pp. 223-225 (1922). Letters to James Madison, Sept. 10 and 12, 1807.

[2] *Louisa County, Virginia, 1743-1814: Where Have All the Children Gone?* (1980), p. 44.

[3] J. B. Minor, *The Minor Family of Virginia* (1923), p. 15. *Va. Mag. Hist. Biog.*, vol. 20, p. 288 (1912).

[4] *Calendar of Virginia State Papers*, vol. 9, p. 402 (1890).

[5] Letters to Peachy R. Gilmer, July 17, 1806 (referring to the death to his wife), February 20, 1807 (mentioning that his law practice is going well), August 22, 1807 (saying that he is very ill and that his sister had recently died): Virginia Historical Society, Mss1 G4216a 179-181.

[6] "The Will of David Yancey," *Louisa County Historical Mag.*, vol. 1, no. 2, pp. 72-74 (Dec. 1969); *Virginia Argus* (Richmond), February 2, 1808; *Enquirer* (Richmond), January 30, 1808.

David Yancey had a brother, Robert, and two sisters, Polly and Eliza, the latter of whom was married to William Kimbrough, but she predeceased her brother, David. [7]

## YANCEY'S REPORTS

David Yancey's reports are found in a small paper booklet that is now in the David Watson Collection in the Library of Congress, MMC 2514, box 2. Yancey was a close personal friend and a close neighbor of Watson in Louisa County. They practiced law in the same part of Virginia, and therefore it is not surprising that Watson had these reports made by his friend and brother at the bar.

This collection of cases was made by David Yancey from his observations in the courtroom no doubt while waiting for his own cases to be called. Some of the information, however, was given to him by others. Yancey does not mention which of these cases he argued himself, but he does refer to several other lawyers: W. Leake, J. Barham, D. Carr, and Brown.

The cases reported are all from the District Court of Charlottesville from April 1804 to April 1806.

## Notes of Decisions of The District Court of Charlottesville commencing April term 1804 and ending [    ] taken by D. Yancey.

Prentis and Carrington were the judges assigned to this District this term, but Prentis was absent from sickness.

### Commonwealth v. Gaines

Presentment for suffering gaming in his house, under the Act of 1797. R.C. [8] 373, § 3, which gives the penalty of $150 to

---

7 "The Will of David Yancey" *supra*.

8 *A Collection of All Such Acts of the General Assembly . . .* (1803). Although the reporter refers to this compilation of statutes, the footnotes will refer to Hening's Statutes and Shepherd's Statutes since these works have been recently reprinted and are thus much more accessible.

any person who will sue for the same. [9] As the Commonwealth is not a person, this penalty cannot be recovered by presentment or information. On this point, several presentments were dismissed both here and at Staunton. (Sic vide R.C. 100, § 5[10], which was insisted on in this case.)

### Black v. Commonwealth

Supersedeas to a judgment for $30 and costs for retailing spiritous liquors without [a] license.

The court has jurisdiction as the amount of [the] judgment and costs are of the value of $33.33 cents. (See R.C. 82, §55 [11]). A defect in the presentment [is] not material nor were the court wrong in refusing to quash it on the motion to show cause. A variance between present[ment] and information [is] immaterial (if it were sufficient to ground an information upon, I presume) as the court might direct an information to be filed without presentment upon affidavit and as the information is sufficient, the presentment is out of [the] question.

### Galt (?) v. William Walker

Debt.

Plea by [the] common bail and issue. The principal defendant died. At [the] trial, [the] common bail offered to enter special bail. The suit abated as to Walker, and the court refused to suffer the common bail to enter himself special bail. Exceptions were taken by W. Leake, attorney, and judgment [was given] against [the] common bail.

### Goodwin and Wife, who was administratrix of Gideon Grantland v. Pauncy Bunch

This was a scire facias to revive a judgment obtained by [the] intestate in the year 1790. [The] defendant, at [the] set-

---

9  Shepherd's Statutes, vol. 2, p. 75.

10  Shepherd's Statutes, vol. 1, p. 18.

11  Hening's Statutes, vol. 13, p. 447.

ting aside [of] the office judgment, plead the Act of Limitations and that [the] scire facias [was] issued more than ten years after judgment and without leave of court. [There was a] demurrer to both pleas, but [the] court directed the plea of [the] act of limitations to be written and that [the] plaintiff should withdraw his demurrer and reply specially and that [the] defendant should demur. [It was said] by the court [that] the action is barred by the Statute of Limitations passed in 1792 [12] although the judgment was rendered prior thereto.

The court [said] the second plea was in abatement, as I was told, but declined deciding it the next day.

### Thomas Barbour v. William Love

A general demurrer is an issuable plea on [the] setting aside [of] an office judgment, but a special demurrer is not, and therefore this demurrer, which states a variance between the declaration and [the] covenant, was not received.

### Hawkins' ex'r v. Barclay's devisees [13]

Debt.

On setting aside [an] office judgment and writ of enquiry, at the trial, [there was] a demurrer stating for cause that the heirs were not joined in the action with the devisees, the declaration stating the latter to be daughters. [It was said] by the court [that] this is a demurrer in abatement and [is] not admissible after [an] office judgment.

Leave was given to withdraw [the] demurrer and plead payment on paying costs.

The judge said the action may be maintained singly (as I was told) against devisees.

---

12  Shepherd's Statutes, vol., p. 98.

13  Later proceedings in this case are reported below and in Watson's reports. Note the connected case Hawkins's Exor's v. Berkley, 1 Va. (1 Wash.) 204 (1793).

## [Anon.] v. Skelton Conard & Co.

Debt.

The defendant John Henderson offered to plead that he was not a partner of Skelton Conard & Co., which was refused as being in abatement and not admissible after [an] office judgment.

### Jefferson qui tam v. Johnson

[There was a] verdict for [the] defendant, and [a] new trial [was] granted as the verdict was against [the] law and [the] evidence manifestly and as the jury had disregarded the advice of the judge to find a special verdict. On [a] motion to reconsider the point, the court said no new trial can be granted in [a] special prosecution where there has been a full and fair trial and no misdirection of the judge although the jury have found a verdict for [the] defendant against [the] law and [the] evidence. Therefore the order for [a] new trial was set aside and judgment [was entered] for [the] defendant.

### [Anon.] v. Morris

[There was a] plea and issue. Afterwards [the] plaintiff demurs. This is a waiver of the issue and admits the facts contained in [the] plea to be true.

### William West for M.A.S. v. James Monroe

Notice [was given] to James Lewis, his agent. [There was a] question as to the legality of the notice. [It was said] by [the] court [that] the notice is insufficient.

### [Anon.] v. [Anon.]

[There was a] supersedeas to [the] judgment of [the] Amherst County Court. The C[ommon] O[rder] was confirmed against [the] principal obligee [?]. At [the] next term, the common bail entered special bail but did not set aside [the] office judgment and plead. The clerk confirmed the judgment against [the] common bail. For this, there was a supersedeas granted, at which this court seemed astonished and quashed the supersedeas and affirmed the judgment.

September term 1804.

Parker and Stuart, judges.

### Gilmer's ex'r. v. Bruce et al.[14]

[A] capias [was] executed on one; [an] alias capias [went] against Bruce; [there was] judgment against the other; [a] delivery bond [was] taken, and [there was] judgment on that. The cause being called, [the] plaintiff moved for judgment for his costs against Bruce.

Judge Stuart said [the] plaintiff has a right to pursue the second defendant till the money be made or the parties changed by a delivery bond. And this being the first term since the delivery bond was taken, [he] dismissed the suit and gave [the] plaintiff judgment for his costs.

### Crawford v. Murrill, late sheriff

A [writ of] capias ad satisfaciendum being issued was executed on [          ],[15] who gave [a] bond for the [prison] bounds. The prisoner was turned over by Hughes, the former sheriff, to Murrill, who discharged him for want of security for prison fees, he being unable to pay them, as was said. Crawford moved against Murrill for the amount of the execution and damages of 15 per cent for a voluntary escape. The previous question whether this sheriff were liable by motion [for judgment], if at all, was moved:

1st. Because the prisioner was not in jail but in the bounds and did not come within the law. R.C.

2nd. That this law did not extend to a succeeding sheriff.

3. That the law had given a remedy by suit. R.C.

---

14  This case was also reported in Watson's reports.

15  Left blank in MS.

4. That when [a] prisoner is in the bounds, the law only requires [the] sheriff to give notice to [the] plaintiff, assign the bond to him, and take out an escape [warrant], but [it] does not subject him to [a] motion [for judgment] for neglect of his duty in this respect.

5. That [the] plaintiff resided out of the county and had no agent in the county. R.C.

The court were of [the] opinion [that] the motion [for judgment] would not lie and that [the] sheriff was not liable by action, [the] prisoner not being in his custody.

### [Anon.] v. [Anon.] [16]

[There was a] motion to quash an execution and delivery bond because the execution was returnable to the district office the first day of a month, which was a Sunday. The court said the law intended a benefit to [the] plaintiff but, in compliance with the opinions of the country, would not require the sheriff to return the execution on Sunday but authorized him to return it the next day without being subject to a fine, and [it] was merely directory to the officer (viz. the clerk) that the execution was neither void nor voidable. And [the court] overruled the motion.

### Hall v. Maupin

[There was a] motion for [a] supersedeas after [an] office judgment against [the] defendant and bail. The bail entered special bail but omitted to set aside the office judgment. The clerk issued [a writ of] execution against the defendant and [the] bail. The county court on motion quashed the execution. The plaintiff excepted to their opinion, moved for, and obtained a supersedeas.

### Barnett v. Chewning

Ejectment.

16 Anon. and Co. v. Jones. This case is also reported in Watson's reports.

The plaintiff claimed under and from [    ] [17] Chewning, to whom his father willed one third of his land, proved by parol evidence a division between the devisees, that his grantor had been in possession since the death of his father, and also proved possession in his grantor's father for more than twenty years. The court said the possession of the father was the possession of the son and his grantee and was sufficient to maintain the title. N.B. the will directed in what manner the land should be descended [?].

## McPherson v. Ross [18]

Covenant.

The covenant was a long settlement of differences between the parties. [The] plaintiff had bound Ross to [keep] the peace, and Ross having broken his recognizance, a scire facias issued. [The] plaintiff agreed, among other things, not to appear when called to the end that the scire facias might not be prosecuted with effect; Ross was to give [the] plaintiff [a] bond and security for his personal safety and make satisfaction in money for certain injuries, of which [the] plaintiff complained.

Judge Stuart thought the consideration immoral and the whole contract void. Judge Parker thought the consideration not immoral and the contract not void and that [the] plaintiff had a right to compound the prosecution. [The] jury [was] equally divided also and [was] withdrawn.

## [Anon.] v. Burnley

Supersedeas.

[The] common bail pleaded. The principal then died, and the bail moved the court to abate the suit, which they did. [The] plaintiff excepted and obtained [a] supersedeas.

---

17  Left blank in the MS.

18  Later proceedings in this case are reported below.

# DAVID YANCEY

April term 1805

John Tyler and Robert White, judges.

## Hawkins' admr. v. Barclay's devisees[19]

Debt on [a] bond.

[There was a] plea [of] payment.

[ ] The defendant holds the affirmative and has a right to open and conclude the cause. The five years five months and eighteen days in the Act of Assembly ought to go to the jury to rebut the presumption of twenty years.

## Commonwealth v. Dixon[20]

Indictment for forgery.

The obligor of the bond forged was not admitted to prove the forgery. [The] court [was] divided. [Judge] Tyler thought the verdict could not be given in evidence in a suit on the bond. [Judge] White thought it could and also that it was the custom of courts to destroy the forged paper, which would prevent suit being brought on it against the obligor. So the witness was not admitted. But the assignor was admitted, the prisoner not being indicted for forging the assignment.

## Medlock's admr. v. Chisholm[21]

Debt on [a] judgment. Devastavit. [?]

The declaration recited the penalty for which the judgment was given without stating the condition. The court refused to let the judgment go in evidence. The plaintiff suffered a nonsuit. And the court set aside the nonsuit on [the] motion of [the] plaintiff's counsel and reinstated the cause.

---

19  Earlier proceedings in this case are reported above.

20  This case is also reported in Watson's reports.

21  This case is also reported in Watson's reports.

## Hart s.p. etc. v. Nelson[22]

Devastavit.

[The] plaintiff declared that by the consideration of the court, he had recovered. The record stated that judgment was confessed for the amount of an award made in the cause wherefore it is ordered by the court etc. [There was an] objection that ordered and considered were not the same and that the latter is essential to a judgment. The court seemed to think the objection [to be] a legal one. But it being suggested to be the mistake of the clerk, a juror was withdrawn, the cause continued, and certiorari awarded.

## [Anon.] v. [Anon.]

Debt.

Judge White [said that] special bail may be given before the appearance day. Judge Tyler assented.

## Woods v. Shields

[This was a] case for goods furnished her before she was married. It was moved by [the] defendant that the debt was extinguished by her marriage and that the action should have been brought against the administrator of her husband, who became liable for her debts by the marriage.

Judge White, who sat alone, said the husband is entitled to his wife's goods if he reduces them into possession during coverture, but if he does not and she survives, the goods survive to her. He is liable for her debts in consequence of his being entitled to her goods. If he be sued for her debt during coverture, he is liable. But if the wife survive, the creditor has his option. For as the right to her goods not reduced into possession during coverture survive to her, the action ought to survive against her also.

---

22 Later proceedings in this case are reported below and in Watson's reports.

April term 1806.

Nelson and Stuart, judges.

### Hart etc. v. Nelson[23]

Devastavit.

There had been a judgment against [the] defendant as administrator of John Nelson quando assetae acciderint. On this judgment, a scire facias issued requiring [the] defendant to appear and say whether assets had come to her hands to pay the debt but not stating that assets had come. On this scire facias, there was [a] judgment by default. Then this action was brought suggesting a devastavit, and the judgment on the scire facias [was] offered as conclusive evidence of assets and the waste there being a return of nulla bona.

But [the] court said [that the] plaintiff must prove assets by other evidence. Nelson [was] absent.

The scire facias did not aver assets. The judgment on it pursued the first judgment, and there must be proof of assets coming since the first judgment. Exceptions [were] taken.

### Davis v. Davis

[This was an action for] devastavit by several jointly on a decree in chancery against [the] administrator for several sums to be paid to the several plaintiffs as legatees. [The] court said they could not maintain the action jointly on a decree in their favor for several sums of money making a total sum of [   ][24].

### C. Peyton v. J. Quarles

[This was an action in] detinue for a Negro purchased by [the] defendant at [a] sheriff's sale and claimed by [the] plain-

23  Earlier proceedings in this case are reported above and in Watson's reports.

24  Left blank in the MS.

tiff under a deed of mortgage from C. L. Lewis, against whom the execution issued, to [the] plaintiff. [The] deed [was] produced by [the] plaintiff, and [there was] proof of delivery of the Negro by Lewis to Peyton. [The] deed [was] proved by one witness but not yet recorded, but the sale took place within eight months after the delivery of the deed. [The] sale [was] forbade by [the] plaintiff, but [there was] no proof that [the] defendant had actual notice of the deed.

[It was said by the] court [that] proof of [the] execution of the deed by one witness at the trial is good, and therefore [it is] not necessary [that] the deed shall go to the jury on such proof because the deed is good between the parties, but [the] plaintiff must prove that [the] defendant had actual notice of the notice within eight months, the deed not being recorded as the law directs.

A witness then said [that] he thought [the] plaintiff mentioned at the sale under what title he claimed but does not know that he showed the deed. Another witness said [the] plaintiff held a paper in his hand and said the Negroes were his.

[The] court said if the deed had been recorded within eight months, it would have availed [the] plaintiff, but not having done this, there must have been notice on the day of [the] sale of the deed.

A witness who was su[mmoned] [?] for the deputy sheriff, who sold the Negroes, who said he thought himself interested, was rejected. The sheriff was indemnified.

### Davis v. Hening

Debt.

[There was an] office judgment against [the] principal, plea by [the] common bail, special bail given, and motion for leave to withdraw the plea for [the] common bail and plead for [the] principal. At the next term after a final judgment against [the] principal, curia advisari vult.[25]

Afterwards [the] court said it was against their own opinion of the law but found from a case cited in the appendix to

T[ucker's edition of] Blackstone[26] that it was the practice of the old General Court, and they felt themselves bound by the precedent in the case cited from [the] General Court [that] after [the] death of [the] common bail who had pleaded, the defendant was allowed to defend his plea.

### John Carn and wife v. Reuben Norvel

Ejectment.

[The] plaintiffs produced a patent dated 1755 to John and William Christian and William Brown. It was admitted [that] the two first died and that the land survived to Brown, that the land was forfeited for nonpayment of quit rents and user [?] and John Christian, son of one of the first named patentees, petitioned for the land as lapsed in 177[ ], and in 1774 the General Court gave judgment in their[27] favor, and the petitioners sold to Gresham, who sold to Powell, whose heirs the lessors of [the] plaintiffs are. No patent issued on the judgment of [the] General Court. [The] defendants contended that the judgment of [the] General Court did not convey the legal title but only a right to enter and obtain a patent and produced [a] patent to [the] defendant dated 1795 for the same land. The entry survey [?] and patent were all subsequent to the judgment of [the] General Court.

[The] plaintiff proved possession [for] twenty-six years prior to 1800 and that he had paid the taxes. [The] plaintiff's counsel contended that land lapsed for nonpayment of quit rents is not waste and unappropriated land especially when a judgment of [the] General Court has been obtained by a petitioner for the land, [and he] cited V.L.E. 1769, p. 148,[28] and that this law pointed out a particular mode of acquiring title

---

25 The court took the case under advisement.

26 St. G. Tucker, *Blackstone's Commentaries*, vol. 3, Appendix, Note C, pp. 48-49 (1803).

27 Sic in MS.

28 *Acts of Assembly Now in Force* . . . (1769). Also in Hening's Statutes, vol. 5, pp. 418-419.

to such lands different from that in which title to waste land was acquired and that the judgment of [the] General Court vested the title, or if not, that they may now as assignees obtain a patent, that there was a difference between the law of 1748[29] and that in Ed. 1733[30].

The court said this land has been once patented and the defendant must show before he reads his patent as evidence that a patent could have been legally obtained for such land, that it was like the case of an escheat patent in which it must be shown that the land was escheated etc., and that the judgment of the General Court did not divest the title of Brown until a patent issued to the petitioner.

Coalter contended for [the] defendant [that] they could not go beyond the grant and that the judgment of the General Court divested Brown's title and vested it in the king for the purpose of regranting generally and not for a particular person, [and] that the petition to the General Court was like an office found.

But the court said the land vested in the king for the purpose of granting to the petitioner and for no other end.

[The] defendant's counsel wished a special verdict, to which [the] plaintiff objected, and the points before stated were urged to prove the propriety on one side and the impropriety on the other.

Christian, a witness, said he had known the land since 1761 when it was in the possession of John Christian, one of the patentees, and so continued till between 1761 and 1765, when John died. The other patentee named Christian died about 1758. There was a settlement on the [   ][31] Brown sent his son to take possession of the land the fall after John's death and

---

29  Hening's Statutes, vol. 5, pp. 418-419.

30  *A Collection of All the Acts of Assembly* . . . (1733), p. 262. Also in Hening's Statutes, vol. 3, p. 526.

31  The page ends here, and some words seem to have been inadvertently omitted in the MS.

continued there till 1772. A petition was presented for the land, and [there was] an agreement between John and Charles Christian (the sons) and Brown to give him 1000 acres of the land not to appear to the caveat. John and Charles came into possession about 1772 and continued till the deed was made to Gresham, [he] found Gresham in possession in 1779, and he continued till he sold to Powell, who held the land till his death, and the tenants of Powell's representatives were in possession after Powell's death. [He] never heard of any adverse possession till Norvel took possession. [The] first tenant claimed under Brown, as he was informed; the others under John and Charles Christian; their tenant was in possession in 1775. In 1777, 1778, 1779 James Gresham held the land in possession.

Burruss, a witness, proved [the] tax [was] paid for the years 1785, 1786, 1787, 1788, [and] 1789. [He] heard Norvel say he did not dispute the payment of the taxes from 1785 to this time. T. Powell, father of [the] wife of [the] lessor of [the] plaintiff, died [in] 1788. [The] defendant's entry was made in 1794 in [the] land office; [there was a] treasury warrant [and] possession in [the] plaintiffs and those under whom they claim from a time prior to 1775 till November 1800 when [the] defendant ousted them.

[A] special verdict was found stating these facts, and judgment without further argument [was given] for [the] plaintiff. And [there was an] appeal.

### Mullins v. Higginbotham

[There was a] motion to quash execution because [the] sheriff returned "former execution executed on a Negro and released by injunction," which appeared to have been obtained in the county court. Another execution issued, and [the] defendant moved to quash it; the injunction in [the] county court had not been dissolved; [the] execution was quashed. It did not appear by [the] sheriff's return in what court the injunction was granted.

The court seemed not disposed to go out of the return and refused to let the sheriff amend at that time because it might injure the plaintiff. The second execution had been levied on [the] defendant's property.

### R. Draffen v. C. L. Thomas

Covenant.

[It was said] by the court [that] a deed or contract referred to in a covenant is made part of it and its stipulations [are] to be performed as if recited.

Robert Lewis devised land to John Thomas and [his] wife for life, remainder to Charles Lewis Thomas, their son. John Thomas sold the land to [the] plaintiff and gave a mortgage to secure a conveyance of 722 acres of land by estimation when C. L. Thomas came of age. C. L. Thomas, when he came of age, executed a deed of bargain sale release and confirmation to [the] plaintiff with [a] general warranty. [The] plaintiff offered to prove the intention and understanding of the parties by parol proof.

But [the] court said you may prove anything out of the deed but not prove or explain the meaning of the deed. [The] court thought that C. L. Thomas was as much bound for a deficiency in the quantity of land [as] John Thomas would have been if he had conveyed etc.

### James Bates v. Robert Rives

Case on an award.

[The] defendant moved that this was no award because it left a part of the matter unsettled saying [the] plaintiff should be allowed for certain work at certain rates when he proved the quantity done and because the arbitrators had exceeded the bounds of their authority in fixing the price of the work by an agreement between [the] plaintiff and defendant which was handed to them by [the] defendant when [the plaintiff] was not present and no previous mention was made by the parties that they were to be governed by that agreement. And when the witness, who was one of the arbitrators, said he should have rated [?] the work higher, [the] court said it was no award. The witness at first said they were to be governed by this agreement which fixed the prices of the work. [The] court said a contract referred to and made part of [the] submission and referred to in an award is part of the award. The witness, then on being further examined (one Metcalf), varied his evidence as above, in consequence of which the agreement was not suffered to be read.

[The] plaintiff suffered [a] nonsuit there being no count but on the award. [There was a] motion to set aside [the] nonsuit. [The] court [said that the] plaintiff must pay the whole costs and may amend his declaration but must not insist on the award again. [The] plaintiff refused [?] to accept of these terms.

### James McPherson v. James D. Ross[32]

Case.

[The] plaintiff had bound [the] defendant to keep the peace, who had forfeited his recognizance, and [a] scire facias had issued. [The] plaintiff claimed compensation for services and for losses sustained by being driven out of employment by [the] defendant. [The] parties came to an agreement, and [the] plaintiff agreed not to appear against [the] defendant on the scire facias, and Ross [was] to pay what [the] plaintiff claimed of him. [The] defendant's counsel moved to suppress the contract as being founded on an immoral consideration and cited 2 Wilson.[33] [The] court withheld the paper from the jury. [There was an] exception and appeal.

Stuart in court.

### [Anon.] v. Brown etc.

Appeal.

A motion [for judgment] had been made on a delivery bond in [the] County Court of Albemarle. The court were di-

32   Earlier proceedings in this case are reported above.

33   Collins v. Blantern, 2 Wilson K.B. 341, 95 Eng. Rep. 847 (C.P. 1767).

vided as to the sufficiency of the notice, and an entry to that effect [was] made on the record. Another notice was given to [the] next court, and judgment [was entered] on [the] delivery bond. [There were] exceptions taken and [an] appeal. J. Barham for [the] appellant contended:

1st. That the first motion was still pending in the County Court.

2d. That the names of the Negroes were not mentioned in the sheriff's return which was "D. Bond taken and forfeited," nor does [the] sheriff say "executed," but the delivery bond states the names of the Negroes and says the property was taken by [the] sheriff.

D. Carr for [the] appellee replied that the first motion was not pending, it not being continued, [and] that it was not necessary to endorse the names of the Negroes on [the] execution unless [they] were sold. [He] cited Echolls v. Graham, 1 Call's Reports[34], and that the delivery bond states the names and says they were taken by the sheriff under the execution. [The] court affirmed the judgment.

### Nailor v. Clarkson

In an action on the case for services rendered, [the] plaintiff was permitted in the County Court of Albemarle to read a sealed instrument of writing without proving the execution of it by the parties. [The] judgment [was] reversed.

### Governor [of Virginia] for William Cannon v. Robert Quarles, sheriff [of] Fluvanna [County]

Debt on [a] sheriff's bond.

In this case, the pleadings were lengthy, and the question urged by [the] defendant's counsel was if an action can be sustained on [a] sheriff's bond for a trespass committed by his deputy in taking one man's property under an execution

---

34 Eckhols v. Graham, 5 Va. (1 Call) 492 (1799).

against another. 1 Washington's Reports 90, Bibb v. Cauthorn,[35] was cited.

The first breach assigned in replication was that [the] sheriff had taken Cannon's property to pay Cocke's debt; and [there was a] demurrer on the ground first stated that this action would not lie.

[The] second breach stated an excessive distress on Cocke's property hired to Cannon, the execution being previously levied on a sufficiency of Cocke's property.

[The] third [was] that [the] sheriff levied execution against Cocke on property which was Cannon's by hire.

4th. [                    ].[36]

[There was a] demurrer to all the breaches assigned.

[The] court said that debt on [a] sheriff's bond will lie for trespass in taking one man's property for another's. The case of Bibb v. Cauthorn covers this case. But [Judge] Stuart said it was not his opinion. [The] demurrer [was] overruled.

2. Cocke's property in Cannon's hands is liable to be taken for Cocke's debts. The reversion of Negroes hired is liable for debt. Cannon cannot complain of excessive distress of Cocke's property. [The] demurrer [was] sustained.

In Douglas,[37] it is said [that] trespass will lie against [a] principal for the act of the deputy. In McCall v. Ruffin[38], it is said [that] there is no necessity for a previous suit against [the] principal before a suit against his securities.

On [the] 3d breach, [the] demurrer [was] sustained.

On [the] 4th, [it was] overruled.

---

35  1 Va. (1 Wash.) 91 (1792).

36  Left blank in the MS.

37  Ackworth v. Kempe, 1 Dougl. 40, 99 Eng. Rep. 30 (K.B. 1778).

38  Call v. Ruffin, 5 Va. (1 Call) 333 (1798).

The court allowed [the] defendant to withdraw [his] demurrers to [the] first and fourth breaches and plead, saying this is the modern practice.

### Jesse Mills v. Hudson's exr.

Case.

John Hudson wrote to A. Ballenger, his son-in-law, that he was to pay £10 per annum for the Negro in his possession to his daughter Mills for ten years if she lived that time or left issue and then Ballenger was to have the Negro. This letter was dated February 1794. [The] jury found that no valuable consideration was paid, that said paper was presented and protested as a bill of exchange about nine years after, that [the] testator devised to his daughter as much as to his other children, and that he conceived himself discharged from this claim. [The] testator devised her £75. Rachel Mills is dead leaving a child.

[The] plaintiff's counsel called it a bill of exchange, said [that] notice was not necessary till the end of ten years, and that unless some loss has happened, notice was in good time. Brown and Nelson [were] for [the] plaintiff.

Carr for [the] defendant [said] this is no bill of exchange. It is an action on the case and profert of a sealed writing, but on the merits, the law is for [the] defendant. It is a gift by a parent to his child of a certain piece of property or of a certain debt, and if the gift proves to be worth nothing, he is not liable to make it good.

Judgment [was] for [the] defendant.

### Commonwealth v. Michie, sheriff of Albemarle

[There was a] presentment for not keeping [the] jail in good order. [The] defendant contended [that a] sheriff was not liable criminally for the act of the jailor and cited 2 Ld. Raymond 1580.[39]

---

[39]  Rex v. Huggins, 2 Ld. Raym. 1574, 1580, 92 Eng. Rep. 518, 522

But [the] court said [that] sheriffs [are] liable for [a] breach of the duties of his office by his deputy not only civilly but penally though not criminally. The jailor or any other person [is] not allowed to be a witness to exculpate himself except in cases of contempt. Upon a rule to show cause, [the] defendant must not deny the facts but confess and avoid them.

### Henderson v. Clarkson

[This was] for dower in a house and lot in the town of Milton. The question was if a widow be entitled to dower in lots laid out for a town by direction of an Act of Assembly[40]. The law establishing the town says nothing about dower but bars all claims under Henderson. J. Barham for [the] defendant cited a case stated by Judge Brooke at the last term, of Beverley, who intermarried with Riddick, where the entail was docked and the estate vested in trustees. The widow failed to recover dower. The case of the heir in entails [and] ad quod damnum in case of mills [and] roads etc. were cited.

Nelson for [the] plaintiff contended [that] the wife's right is vested and cannot be divested, that her right is not affected by docking entails, that the interest of the heir was different, that it was not vested might be defeated by [a] fine and recovery, and that an equivalent was recited in lieu but the wife's right was vested and not to be defeated but in [the] manner prescribed by Act of Assembly which is positive. The wife is a purchaser. 2 B.C. 132, 2 B.A. 337, 382. In Beverley's Case, the land was vested in commissioners, who sold it and made the conveyance, but no conveyance [was] executed by [the] husband or wife. This law [was] passed before the Revolution to dock an entail; £1500 [was] to be applied to pay debts and the balance to be laid out in lands and slaves, [ ] of which should be females and be settled on the family.

(K.B. 1730).

40    Hening's Statutes, vol. 13, pp. 87-89.

[The] court gave no opinion. They said they must see the law establishing the town.

### Fox v. Cary

Caveat; Special verdict.

Fox purchased Spencer Rayfield's survey which had been settled thirty years before the entry. Judgment [was given] for [the] caveator.

### Richard Morris v. Turner Anderson

Case.

Eight persons joined in the purchase of a Negro man black-smith named Cobb for the purpose of emancipating him so soon as he had paid the purchase [price] by his labor. Six of them gave £20 each, and two gave £10 each. It was under-stood that Cobb should work at Morris's shop. Morris found a shop and [　] tools, food etc. Anderson had work done at the shop, for which this suit was brought. Cobb continued in Morris's shop two years without any special agreement. Morris allowed £28 a year for his work toward paying the pur-chase money and settled with the partners, except [the] defendant, on these terms, and all but three certified that they were satisfied. [The] defendant's counsel contended this was a partnership transaction and that the action was miscon-ceived.

The court said [that] it was a partnership formed for a par-ticular purpose, with whom did Morris make a contract or agreement to give £28 a year for the services of the Negro and not with the Negro. He could not, not with the other partners. There is no evidence of this. Morris is entitled to compensa-tion for tools, food, etc. furnished, and the balance should go to the partners to pay the advances made by them. If Morris can prove a contract with the partners to take the Negro at a particular price, he may do so, and then the action is sustain-able. Otherwise he must account with them, they being enti-tled to the services of the Negro. But a court of chancery alone is competent to settle these complicated accounts.

It was then proved that Cobb went to work in Morris's shop by consent of the partners, but that no particular bargain was made, that £28 was more than he had hired for some years before, that it was agreed [that] fifty per cent should be added to the price of work done for the partners, that no accounts were rendered till [the] end of [the] second year, nor did [the] witness ever hear on what terms the Negro worked but supposed from what he had heard that he was to have the benefit of his work and never expected to have any dispute, that Cobb had hired one year at £26 and two years at £27. Cobb [was] about sixty-two years old at this time.

[The] court then said [that] the whole of the partners could not have sued Col. Morris at common law, that unless the jury think a special contract [is] proved between Col. Morris and the other partners, the action is not sustainable.

[The] jury [was] divided.

# Index

The references below provide the number of the page on which the case begins and in parentheses the number of the case on the page. For instance, the fourth case on page five is referenced 5(4).